EVA B

D1478130

To Serve and Protect: Communicating in Law Enforcement in Canada

Lucy Valentino
Humber College Institute of
Technology and Advanced Learning

NELSON EDUCATION

NELSON EDUCATION

To Serve and Protect: Communicating in Law Enforcement in Canada

by Lucy Valentino

Associate Vice President, Editorial Director:
Evelyn Veitch

Editor-in-Chief, Higher Education:
Anne Williams

Publisher:
Cara Yarzab

Acquisitions Editor:
Bram Sepers

Senior Marketing Manager:
David Tonen

Developmental Editor:
Liisa Kelly

Photo Researcher:
Jessie Coffey

Permissions Coordinator:
Jessie Coffey

Production Service:
Macmillan Publishing Solutions

Copy Editor:
Elizabeth Phinney

Proofreader:
Dianne Fowlie

Indexer:
Dave Luljak

Senior Production Coordinator:
Ferial Suleman

Design Director:
Ken Phipps

Managing Designer:
Franca Amore

Interior Design:
Peggy Rhodes

Cover Design:
Johanna Liburd

Cover Image:
© iStockphoto.com/ Frances Twitty

Compositor:
Macmillan Publishing Solutions

Printer:
Transcontinental

For permission to use material from this text or product, submit all requests online at www.cengage.com/permissions. Further questions about permissions can be emailed to permissionrequest@cengage.com

Every effort has been made to trace ownership of all copyrighted material and to secure permission from copyright holders. In the event of any question arising as to the use of any material, we will be pleased to make the necessary corrections in future printings.

Library and Archives Canada Cataloguing in Publication

Valentino, Lucy, 1952-
    To serve and protect : communicating in law enforcement in Canada / Lucy Valentino.

Includes index.
ISBN 978-0-17-650125-9

1. Communication in police administration--Textbooks.
2. Police reports--Textbooks.
I. Title.

HV7936.C79V34 2009   808'.066363
C2009-900078-4

ISBN-13: 978-0-17-650125-9
ISBN-10: 0-17-650125-8

Contents

Preface

As I sit down to write these acknowledgements, I am amazed at the number of people I should thank—amazed because the journey that has brought me to write this textbook has been filled with such wonderful experiences and so many fine companions. I have had the privilege to teach those wanting to be police officers and those who are serving in many capacities in several police services. My Police Foundations students have been the guinea pigs for much of this material—I thank them for their energy, enthusiasm, and honesty. I thank those colleagues who have also piloted portions of this work in their Police Foundations classes: Hugh O'Donnell, Irene Kouretsos, Sarah Armenia (who brought the article in Chapter One on art and policing to my attention), and Brad Reed. I thank those practising officers and civilian members of police services who have sat in my class on sunny weekends and foul, and then week after week have valiantly worked through online assignments after a full day at work—or before a long night. I have learned so much from all of them, and I am grateful.

As I teach, I often think of my Uncle Tim, retired captain from the Rochester (N.Y.) Police Department. Officer Timothy L. Jackson earned two degrees while serving full time—he spent well over a decade pursuing higher education. Thanks, Uncle Tim, for sharing your experiences with me.

I thank as well the professors with whom I teach or have taught in the Police Leadership Program: Robin Wilson, Stephen Nancoo, Rick DeFacendis, and Fred Kaustenin. Each has given me a window into a different area of knowledge, and I've enjoyed working as part of a team with them. I also thank the affable John Kelly, who has sat through more of my classes than I have (or maybe just feels that way), and the rest of the Toronto Police team. I thank Pamela Mitchell for her unflappableness and utter reliability. Jane Russ has been a constant source of common sense and good humour. I thank Joe Aversa for his encouragement of my forays beyond the usual bounds of Communications teaching, and Ian Smith for his frequent kind words.

Somehow a thank-you to Frank Trovato seems inadequate to express my appreciation for the difference he has made in police education. He believes passionately in the value of higher education for police officers, and works tirelessly to make that education an achievable goal for serving members. It is a privilege to be his colleague.

I thank in a special way the students who have allowed me to use their work in this textbook. It is so important for Police Foundation students to hear from those on the force how significant writing is in policing, and to have the opportunity to see written work by actual officers. These officers are helping to mold the future by sharing their writing.

I owe a great debt of thanks to the professionals at Nelson Education Ltd. who helped make this text come together. Liisa Kelly, my Developmental Editor, has never learned the phrase "We can't do it." Everything I asked for, she found a way to do. I thank her for her good pedagogical sense, as well as for her enormous patience. I would also like to thank the following Nelson Education Ltd. staff for their fine work: Cara Yarzab, Publisher; Bram Sepers, Acquisitions Editor; David Tonen, Senior Marketing Manager; Ferial Suleman, Production Coordinator; Susan Calvert, Director of Content and Media Production; Franca Amore, Managing Designer; Johanna Liburd, Designer; Vicki Gould, Director of Asset Management Services; Jessie Coffey, Permissions Coordinator; Elizabeth Phinney, Copy Editor; and Dianne Fowlie, Proofreader.

Additionally, I would like to thank the following reviewers:

Tony Altomare	Centennial College
Kelly Bramwell	Sheridan College
Rick Collett	Seneca College
Dianna McAleer	Algonquin College
Andrew Stracuzzi	Fanshawe College

This text is dedicated to my husband Vince. Please wear your seatbelt.

About the Author

 Dr. Lucy Valentino has over twenty years' experience in the Ontario college system. She has developed and taught a wide variety of composition, workplace writing, critical thinking, liberal arts, and ESL courses throughout her teaching career. She was Chair of the English Department at Centennial College for over a decade, and then was Centennial's Dean responsible for English, General Education, and faculty professional development. At Centennial she received two Board of Governors' Awards—one for innovation and one for academic Leadership—as well as an NISOD Teaching Excellence Award. She joined the Humber College Institute of Technology and Advanced Learning in the School of Liberal Arts in the fall of 2005. In addition to teaching diploma students in Police Foundations and other Social and Community Services programs, she teaches veteran police officers at both the diploma and degree level. She is the author of *Handle with Care: Communicating in the Human Services Field in Canada*, currently in its fourth edition.

Introduction

I have the good fortune to teach not only students who hope to go into law enforcement, but also practising police officers. My institution operates two programs for law enforcement professionals that are unique in Canada, and perhaps the world. Practising police officers can gain a college diploma and then a university degree through an innovative combination of in-class and online learning. I teach the writing portion of both the diploma and degree programs, and so am lucky enough to have a window on the actual world of policing and the role that writing plays for police officers in Canada. What I have learned from these practising police officers underlies this text.

The first thing I have learned is how important writing is in policing. Here are a few comments from my students:

> I believe that writing is one of the most important jobs in my career.... We use our reports to not just communicate the details of what occurred, but also to help us get a conviction in court....

> ... It all comes down to how you communicate on paper. You can have a warrant that is perfectly laid out, but if no one understands what you are describing and what your point is, the warrant is worth nothing, as it will never get signed off by a Justice of the Peace.

> The ability to communicate on paper in the police service is vital to ensure that the right message is being put forward without any confusion.

Writing skills are important at every level of a policing organization, from a street-level constable through superintendents, inspectors, and the chief of police. What is needed may change with various positions in the organization, but the ability to learn from others and to adapt to new writing situations is crucial. My students have shared with me their experiences as they progressed through their policing organizations, and as they faced new writing challenges. For the most part, there was very little formal training in new writing tasks. They were successful with those tasks because they had developed a habit of mind in regard to writing: learn the purpose of the writing task, think about the audience, pay attention to the context, get feedback, and learn from others. These things are what all good writers do; police officers are no different.

This text is built on the philosophy that writing well is an ongoing process of learning and re-learning. The learning process includes the development of specific skills and abilities, and involves adapting to one's circumstances. Writing theorists speak of being able to use different registers, different ways of writing, different vocabulary, in order to suit a particular audience. The ability to think through what is needed in a particular situation is crucial. This text aims to give students practice in negotiating different writing situations to help develop this crucial skill.

Chapter 1 provides an introduction to the writing skills that someone new to policing needs to develop: the ability to observe carefully; the ability to describe precisely and accurately; and the ability to make order out of chaos by giving a logical narrative structure to events that may at first appear to be a jumble, but that can reveal their meaning to someone who puts the puzzle pieces together.

> One of the most challenging aspects to writing on the job is [taking] what can be a complex problem and writing it in a simple way, so that others can easily understand it but yet at the same time trying to get all the relevant points out to the audience.

The following three chapters allow the reader to develop an understanding of the context of police writing and of the many ways the raw material captured by an officer is used. All police officers record their daily activities in notebooks. The material in officers' notebooks forms the basis for various reports, and those data inform the work of crime analysts and the decisions of police executives. Twenty-first century policing is proactive and intelligence-led. We will take a look at how the material in the notebook underlies the activities of an entire policing and legal system, and is crucial in those systems' success.

Chapters 5 through 9 preview the types of writing needed as one progresses in a policing service. Chapter 5 looks at internal police communication using memos written by my students as examples of how situations might be dealt with in writing. Chapter 6 turns to the subject of communicating with the public, considers the purposes of that communication, and explores how that communication might be different from internal communication, not only in format but in approach. Chapter 7 looks at a different way of communicating with the public, through brochures and flyers. Chapter 8 discusses graphics that might be used in memos, letters, or reports. Chapter 9 moves back to internal communication, turning to a specific writing task, that of the business case. As in most organizations, there are limited resources in police services; that is, not enough money, staff, or time to accomplish everything that could be done. These resources are competed for and allocated on the basis of the business case. This chapter examines the process of developing and presenting a business case.

Chapter 10 looks at the writing skills needed by those officers who pursue higher education. How does writing in college or university differ from the writing done on the job by police officers? What is the context for writing in an academic institution? What are the purposes of that writing and what are the typical approaches and format? How is academic writing documented in an academic program such as Justice Studies?

Finally, the text closes with three appendices. Appendix A is a brief introduction to résumés and cover letters. Appendix B discusses some issues of grammar and mechanics that some-times surface in the writing of both inexperienced and experi-enced writers, while Appendix C provides a guide to the spelling of frequently confused sound-alike words.

Each chapter in the text closes with "Explorations," tasks that can be done individually or in groups. Here is your first set of Explorations.

EXPLORATIONS

Intro.1 Take a look at the websites of police organizations in your area of Canada. What is on the website? What can you learn about the philosophy and practice of policing in Canada from what you see?

Intro.2 Look at the following policing website links:

www.police.saskatoon.sk.ca/index.php?loc=recruiting/profile_policeofficer.php

www.city.vancouver.bc.ca/police/recruiting/home.htm

www.torontopolice.on.ca/careers/

What can you learn about the skills expected in a successful applicant to those policing services?

Chapter 1

Foundational Skills for Police Writing

...I first started to learn how to do [police] writing from my coach officer when I first started in my career. He explained to me that when doing a report you have to imagine that you are painting a picture, so that when someone reads your report they understand what is happening.

As we will see in the next chapter, writing in policing has many functions and purposes. The writing an officer does may be read by many audiences: fellow officers, criminal investigation branch detectives, defence lawyers, Crown Attorneys, and so on. In some ways, the officer is the eyes and ears of the justice system. What she or he observes and learns must be conveyed clearly and accurately to others. As the practising police officer states above, the reader of any report must gain a clear picture of a given incident, and it is the officer's job to paint that picture. This chapter will present the foundational skills that allow an officer to paint a clear, vivid, accurate picture for the reader.

Writing a Description

The first skill we'll look at is attention to detail when writing a description. Take a look at the following picture. Imagine this young boy has gone missing, and you need to broadcast an alert. How would you describe him so that he could be identified easily?

Source: Courtesy of Joe Valentino

You would mention his gender, age, race, height, weight, hair colour and type (long, short, straight, wavy, curly). You would also mention what he was last seen wearing in as much detail as possible. Your description might look something like this:

Amber Alert!

Your Police Service is asking the public's help in locating Michael Jenkins ("Mikey"). Mikey is a three-year-old Caucasian boy, approximately 3 feet tall weighing 60 pounds. Mikey has thick straight light blonde hair cut short over the ears with full bangs. He was last seen wearing royal blue cotton pants, a long-sleeved turtleneck shirt under a black and blue patterned sweater and black dress shoes. He disappeared on March 10, 2008. Anyone with information or who may have seen this boy is asked to call Crimestoppers at 1-800-xxx-xxxx.

Using Precise Language

In police writing, care must be taken to use precise language, avoiding terms that might mean different things to different people. For example, what if a witness said a suspect fleeing the scene was "tall"? I am 5 feet 1 inch, while my son-in-law is six foot three. "Tall" means something different to each of us. Or what about someone's weight? Someone who is slim to one person might be heavy-set to another. It's important to use precise language to replace vague terms, even though that "precise" language might include approximations (e.g., "approximately 5 feet 7 inches tall and weighing about 150 pounds").

Descriptions might be written of missing persons, suspects, or victims. Choose one of the following photos. Imagine that the person in the photo is a suspect, a victim, or a missing person. Write a detailed description of the person that could be used to identify him or her.

Source: Handy Widiyanto/Shutterstock

Source: Gelpi/Shutterstock

Source: Ramzi Hachicho/Shutterstock

Source: John Wollwerth/Shutterstock

Source: Elena Ray/Shutterstock

Source: Konstantin Sutyagin/Shutterstock

Source: iofoto/Shutterstock

Source: Tony Wear/Shutterstock

Foundational Skills for Police Writing **13**

Source: Juriah Mosin/Shutterstock

Source: Glenda M. Powers/Shutterstock

Source: Lev Olkha/Shutterstock

Source: iofoto/Shutterstock

Source: Ray Yany/Shutterstock

Source: Yuri Arcurs/Shutterstock

An officer needs not only to describe people; details of crime and accident scenes must also be clear and precise. Look at the following accident photo. What do you notice? Describe the car as precisely as you can. What type of car is it? How many doors? What type of wheels and wheel covers? Describe the damage.

Source: Pakhnyushcha/Shutterstock

Look at these car accident scenes. Describe what you see in detail. Recreate for the reader a vivid picture of what you observe.

Source: Sapsiwai/Shutterstock

Source: Jack Dagley Photography/Shutterstock

Source: Samuel Acosta/Shutterstock

Source: Lori Martin/Shutterstock

Source: Vuk Vukmirovic/Shutterstock

Source: Maria Dryfhout/Shutterstock

Source: Steve Estvanik/Shutterstock

Source: Baloncici/Shutterstock

Source: Rafa Fabrykiewicz/Shutterstock

Describe what you see in the following photos. Can you tell what has been discovered by officers in the first picture? Look carefully at the plants.

Source: Solid Web Designs LTD/Shutterstock

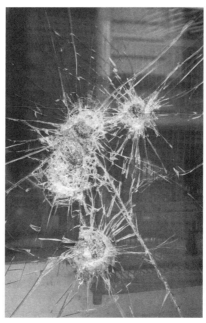

Source: Anyka/Shutterstock

Source: Rafa Fabrykiewicz/Shutterstock

Describe these scenes precisely. The first is a bus shelter that has been vandalized, the second, an abandoned factory, and the rest, examples of graffiti vandalism.

Source: Andrei Nekrassov/Shutterstock

Source: Werner Stoffberg/Shutterstock

Source: Sarah Johnson/Shutterstock

Source: Sean Gladwell/Shutterstock

Source: Emin Kuliyev/Shutterstock

Source: Paul Maguire/Shutterstock

Source: Sean Gladwell/Shutterstock

Source: Emin Kuliyev/Shutterstock

Developing Observational Skills

The article below describes an innovative program run by the New York City Police Department in collaboration with the Frick Art Gallery in New York City. The program uses paintings to develop officers' observational skills. Two of the paintings, *The Death of Marat* and *Las Meninas*, discussed in the article "Did You Notice Their Guns," can be viewed online at www.bc.edu/bc_org/avp/cas/his/CoreArt/art/neocl_dav_marat.html and www.museodelprado.es/en/ingles/collection/on-line-gallery/on-line-gallery/zoom/1/obra/the-family-of-felipe-iv-or-las-meninas/oimg/0/.

Look carefully at the paintings as you read the article. See if you can notice the details being discussed. What else do you see in each painting?

Did You Notice Their Guns?

Even New York's finest can miss the crucial details. It's a matter of needing to 'see' better—a skill they now hone at art class. SIMON HOUPT joins in and discovers why everyone from cops to biologists are taking a close look at the masters.

SIMON HOUPT
NOVEMBER 26, 2005

NEW YORK—On the second floor of a rich man's palace on Fifth Avenue the other day, two dozen New York Police Department officers sat stone-faced around a boardroom table, sipping their morning coffee and staring at a picture of a crime scene. Cops in this city are used to grisly pictures, but this was something unusual, and they were having trouble figuring out exactly what they were seeing: A man lying prone in a bathtub, bleeding from a wound beneath his right clavicle—his head wrapped in what looks like a turban, his right hand hanging almost to the floor— grips a feather pen. His left hand holds a piece of paper.

"Okay, we have blood on a wound—we don't know if it's self-inflicted or from someone else," announces a woman at the front of the room, pointing with a laser. "Where else do we see blood?" She parrots the responses that come back to her. "On the sheets, right. On the floor." She pauses. "Is he dead?" Silence. The cops are uncertain, and besides, they're at a disadvantage: They have no way of knowing that the painting they are looking at is called *The Death of Morat*.

But then, none of the 24 officers had ever before visited the Frick, a jewel box of a museum boasting more than 1,100 paintings, sculptures and decorative arts from Western Europe stretching from the Renaissance to the 19th century. The bulk of the collection was bequeathed by Pittsburgh coke and steel magnate Henry Clay Frick.

Frick built this stone mansion to house the collection and died in 1919 in the former bedroom known as the Walnut Room, where the police have gathered.

Today wouldn't really count as a real visit to the Frick, either, since the police wouldn't take in any of the museum's Rembrandts, Corots, Gainsboroughs, Whistlers or Turners, and would get to look hard at only one of the collection's three Vermeers.

Furthermore, the day's goal was not art appreciation. "If you know the name of the artist or the name of the painting, I don't want to hear it!" says the instructor, Amy Herman, the museum's curator of education and the woman who developed the program. "I'm looking at who, what, where, why and when. I want to make you better observers and better communicators."

Welcome to NYPD: The Blue Period. For almost two years now, the Frick has been running a program with the police department that brings captains into the museum for a few hours to test and hone their observational skills. It was inspired by a program for students at Yale University's medical school which has spawned a number of copycat initiatives around the United States. A study submitted by Yale faculty, and published in the September, 2001, edition of the Journal of the American Medical Association, indicated that students' observational performance was significantly increased by spending a few hours looking at representational paintings.

Observation is supposed to be a primary skill of both law-enforcement officers and physicians, but, as Herman explained in an interview: "If you do something day in and day out, you get used to it and you lose your edge—and you're not as sharp. You're looking at the same things over and over and over again. When you're asked to do that in a little different context, it's a little disarming."

After studying three paintings together, the class descends to the museum's main floor, where they are split into six groups, each assigned a work of art to analyze. After five minutes of discussion, the groups are required to explain the painting to their colleagues. The pieces range from the enigmatic domestic scene of Vermeer's *Mistress and Maid*, in which a servant with a note interrupts a rich woman (is it from her lover, perhaps?) to El Greco's raucous *Purification of the Temple,* in which Jesus drives away the young sinners while aged believers watch expectantly.

Standing by Claude Lorrain's *The Sermon on the Mount*, in which Christ is preaching from the top of Mount Tabor, one sergeant says it seems a good idea to take cues from people in the foreground at the scene who are looking up at the tiny figures in the distance. "If I can relate this to the job," he says, "you pull up on the scene and your first observation is, there's a group of people standing up, looking up there, and you're like: Okay, that's him, right there, there's the jumper." The other cops chuckle: Jesus as a jumper. Herman fixes the student with a smile and says, "You just made my day."

The fact that interacting with art can have beneficial effects beyond offering pleasure or enlightenment is well-chronicled. Exposure to Picasso and Matisse can help patients with Alzheimer's disease keep their memories sharp. Music study during childhood is widely believed to help the brain form neural pathways that assist math and science skills. Prison inmates encouraged to express themselves through painting or music are considered to be less susceptible to negative peer pressure, and less prone to violence.

But professionals are also increasingly using fine art in unorthodox fashions to help improve and alter the way they approach their work.

At the California Institute of Technology in Pasadena, David Kremers is a conceptual artist in biology. "What's happening now is that scientists collect more data than humans can actually perceive," says Kremers. Using the three-dimensional brushstroke techniques of different Impressionist painters, he helps laboratory scientists translate their work into so-called "visualizations" of data, which allow for more intuitive comprehension of the results.

Kremers looks to van Gogh's brushstrokes, which tend to be individualistic: Monet's, which are usually layered on top of one another; and Cézanne's more complex technique, which creates planes of colour through overlapping brushstrokes.

One such study involved tracking the brains of mice as they developed encephalitis lesions. The key variable to track was the relationship between the cells, which is hard to quantify. "Essentially, we discovered that it's a complex, dynamic, multidimensional problem," says Kremers. They plotted the data on what scientists call a 3×3 matrix, tracking the development of the brain cells using nine different axes.

"Nobody really knows how to make pictures of something like that," he continues, "so in this particular case, we used Impressionist painting as a starting point to build a series of computer-generated, mathematically weighted libraries of brushstrokes that could be modeled into 2-D. You would end up with a picture that people could actually point to and say: this is where the lesions will form.

"This is something which science couldn't do on its own, and art couldn't do on its own," he adds.

Art is also helping those in other fields of science see differently. The Frick, which also runs a program with the Weill-Cornell Medical College, modeled its program on one created for first-year students at the Yale University School of Medicine, where students work on their observational skills by spending a few hours at the Yale Center for British Art during a doctor-patient encounter course.

Now in its eighth year, the program began after the YCBA's curator of education, Linda Friedlaender, observed a cancer patient's bedside encounter with a less-than-sensitive medical resident. "You can learn a lot about a patient when you walk into their room: What is the state of their physical hygiene? Are they combing their hair? Do they even have a comb? Did they receive any cards? Any flowers? Have they had visitors? How might that affect their mental state?"

Friedlaender developed the program with Dr. Irwin Braverman, a professor of dermatology at Yale. "When a medical student looks at a patient, the only thing they see are the things that are totally abnormal— because all the normal features are filtered out," says Braverman. "In ordinary life, if you didn't filter out the normal features, you wouldn't be able to walk six feet in the day." But in a discipline such as dermatology, students have to be able to observe the most subtle differences in skin tone and texture that might, on close inspection, reveal a pattern related to disease.

This year, the new dean at the Yale School of Management, Joel Podolny, asked the YCBA to design an orientation program for incoming MBA students. "For managers, it is especially important to be able to make inferences about the social terrain," he wrote in a memo outlining his interest in the program. "When they walk into an organization, they will quickly need to be able to size up the culture, the intentions, and the status hierarchy: Who is respected, who is not? Who should they listen to? What are the dos and don'ts? Who's lying, who's telling the truth?"

Furthermore, by analyzing the paintings in groups, students learn that everyone comes to a painting with a different breadth of life experience, and therefore a different perspective on what they are observing.

"One of the traditional venues of art," says David Kremers, "is coming up with new forms of perspective, and I think in many ways that's what these programs are doing, helping people from other disciplines to see things from a new perspective."

And then he points to a quote from Marcel Proust to help articulate the benefit that art and artists can offer cops, doctors, lab scientists, business managers and many others: "The real voyage of discovery consists not in seeing new landscapes, but in having new eyes."

'Where are we? What are we looking at? What's happening?'

During the Frick program, detectives are shown a slide of *Las Meninas* by Velasquez. What's going on in the painting? Listen in on their observations, guided by Amy Herman, curator of education:

"There's a man in the back. What's he doing? Painting, right. How do we know? Paintbrush, palette, we see the back of the canvas. There's a clue that tells you exactly what he's painting. The mirror? Who's in the mirror? A man and a woman. They're where you are. Describe the relationship between the little girl and the person next to her. They're arguing? What about their body language says they're arguing? The one in the white dress doesn't want to hear what the other one is saying? How do we know? How do you act when you don't want to hear someone? Right: turn your head.

"Now, what's the other one doing that tells you she's trying to talk to her? Okay: pleading, holding her hand. Her body language is: down on her knees. She's saying, 'C'mon, work with me, get back in the picture. A brat? Does this little girl look like a brat?

"I don't know. People frequently think she's the subject of the painting. The actual subject is the king and queen back here, and this little kid maybe ran off the set.

"Okay, what's going on over here on the right? Right, the person here is kicking the dog. See her foot? . . . And who's this? Dwarf, did you say? Is that an adult or a child? Probably an adult, if you look at her facial features. And this one to the left? She's curtseying? Maybe she's getting ready to go on her knees to say: 'C'mon!' Or, also, I could interpret it to say she's picking up her skirts to walk out of there . . . and there's a guy in the back. Is he going or coming? Looks like he's leaving.

"He's got one foot on the upper step, one foot on the lower step. But something caught his attention to draw him back into the room. You're right, he might be entrusted with the little girl's care . . . and can everybody see there's a nun back here? And then there's a guy next to her.

"Where are they, what's the whole setting? You say a studio? A gallery? A museum? Yeah, could be a room in the palace. We don't know. What I want you to do is raise the question: Where are we? What are we looking at? What's happening? Where are we in the painting? Did something just happen when the painting was painted?"

Source: Reprinted with permission from *The Globe and Mail*.

In the Explorations section at the end of this chapter you'll be asked to look at the other paintings mentioned in this article to help hone your observational skills. Practising these skills is essential for a police officer.

Why Are These Skills Important?

An example of the importance of detailed observational skills can be seen in a movie your teacher may show you or that you might watch on your own. *12 Angry Men* recreates a jury's deliberations in a murder trial. At first the case seems open-and-shut. Everyone but one juror is convinced the young man on trial is guilty. However, after looking carefully at the evidence and recreating the details of the alleged offense, the jury realizes that the case is not as open-and-shut as it first appeared. The officers who originally investigated the case missed small details and inconsistencies; that sloppy use of observational skills could have led to an innocent person being executed for murder. Inadequate observational skills can lead not only to the guilty going free, but to the innocent being unjustly condemned.

Practising These Skills: Five-Minute Mystery

Critical thinking and noting inconsistencies are necessary skills that can be practised. Read the following short story from the book *Five-Minute Mysteries* by Ken Weber. (The solution to this mystery is provided at the end of the chapter.)

An Early Morning Murder at 13 Humberview

POLICE CONSTABLE MICHAEL CALEDON PICKED his way gingerly around the piles of gravel and dirt and dust-covered debris strewn about by the road repair crew. Buffing his black shoes to the proper wattage each morning was his least favorite activity and he had no intention of wasting the effort in his first call of the day. He'd parked the patrol car farther away than necessary for the same reason: to keep it clean. When the crew started up at—he looked at his watch—seven o'clock, only nine minutes away, there would be plenty of dirt and noise. He'd seen this bunch move in yesterday to rip up the street.

So complete was his concentration that he found himself on the little flagstone walk at 13 Humberview before he realized it. That surprise, coupled with his sudden awareness that the old lady was sitting on the porch waiting for him, must have showed on his face, for Mrs. Van Nough explained very sweetly:

"I always have my coffee on the porch in this nice weather. Sometimes I even get out before the sun is over those trees. We'll have to go inside today, though; there's not much point in being out here when they start." She waved at the silent machinery on the street. "What do you take in your coffee, young man?"

Michael used the three short strides up the walk to gather himself.

"Good morning." He held out his hands. "I'm here to get...."

"What do you take in your coffee? I have some muffins too, that my neighbour made."

Michael didn't drink coffee, but how did he say no to such a nice old lady?

"Uh ... just half a cup, please, and mild, lots of milk." That was how.

"Excuse me, then. I'll be right back." Mrs. Van Nough got up, shuffled over to the screen door and went inside.

Michael was having real trouble controlling his surprise. The lady was not behaving at all like a bereaved widow. Four days earlier, in fact at just this time—his watch now said 6:54—her husband had been shot in their bed. He was also surprised by how well she spoke. Mrs. Van Nough was deaf, at least according to Sergeant Cosman. Michael had been sent because he was the best on the force at signing. So far, that skill had been entirely superfluous.

His surprise was not diminished in the least when Mrs. Van Nough came back out the door saying:

"No doubt you're wondering how we're able to communicate so easily? Well, I wasn't always deaf. Not until my accident two years ago. Here's your coffee, Constable. I can sign. Are you the one they said would come because you can sign? There's not much need. I'm pretty good at lips. You get good. You have to. Besides, everybody always says the same things to old ladies anyway!"

Her smile grew even sweeter. Michael was so charmed he was almost able to ignore the taste of coffee.

"My other little trick," she lowered her voice conspiratorially, "now don't you tell anybody, Constable." Her smile grew wider and even more irresistible. "My other little trick is, I do all the talking! People don't mind if old ladies prattle on, now do they?

"Now you want to know all about poor Alvin, don't you? I don't know why. I told those other nice policemen everything. Poor Alvin. We were only married three years, you see. He was my third husband."

Without realizing it, Michael bit into a second muffin. He didn't say a word, as Mrs. Van Nough continued.

"It happened when I was having my coffee here, just like this. It was a beautiful day, one of those extra-special summer days. You know, clear, quiet, warm. Of course I couldn't hear the shot, so poor Alvin...."

With a raucous cough, the first of the diesel engines started out on the street, followed by another, then a third, filling the air with a blend of aggressive clatter. The operators held the throttles open, not just to warm up their machines, but also to ensure that everyone in hearing distance would be awake to appreciate their efforts.

Mrs. Van Nough winced. The early morning breeze had brought the exhaust fumes onto the porch.

"Come," she shouted over the din. "We'll go inside. Would you carry the muffins?"

Michael picked up the plate and followed her. How, he thought to himself, how on earth am I going to tell Sergeant Cosman that such a sweet old lady is a liar?

What has tipped Michael Caledon to the realization that Mrs. Van Nough may not be all she pretends?

Source: "An Early Morning Murder at 13 Humberview" from *Five-minute Mysteries* #6. Copyright © 2006 by K.J. Weber Limited 1988, 2006. All rights reserved. Reprinted by permission of Firefly Books Ltd.

Practising These Skills: Scrambled Occurrence

The final type of writing task is one that several police services use as part of their applicant-testing process. It can be thought of as a scrambled occurrence. The applicant is given all the required details of an event (and perhaps a few irrelevant ones as well), and asked to recreate the occurrence in several paragraphs (some tests refer to this as a short essay). In order to do this successfully, the writer must first make order out of the chaos before he or she even begins to write. The writer must painstakingly recreate the occurrence for himself or herself before being able to write it up clearly and coherently for a reader. Try to do this with the following occurrence. These sentences are deliberately given in a scrambled order. Sort the occurrence out for yourself, and then write several paragraphs that give the reader a clear picture of what happened. You do not need to use the exact words of the sentences given here, but you cannot change any facts. Draw logical conclusions from those facts.

Scrambled Occurrence Exercise

1. James Street runs south of West Hill Road.
2. Witness Phyllis O'Meara is at the scene when you arrive.
3. After crossing West Hill Road Phyllis O'Meara and Kisco turned west.
4. Roads are dry.
5. The Toyota Camry has a smashed driver side door.
6. James Street is a two-lane street.
7. Dominion Avenue runs north from West Hill Road.
8. It is February 25, 2008.
9. Phyllis O'Meara was returning from walking her dog, Kisco.
10. The air bag of the Hyundai Accent has deployed.
11. A black cube van is parked illegally at the corner of James Street and West Hill Road
12. Phyllis turned around when she heard a crash.
13. There is a Hyundai Accent in the left eastbound lane.
14. West Hill Road is a four-lane street.
15. The Hyundai Accent waited at the intersection of Dominion Avenue and West Hill Road for Phyllis O'Meara and Kisko to cross before pulling into the left-hand lane going eastbound.
16. There is a red Toyota Camry in West Hill Road across the eastbound left lane and partially in the westbound right lane.
17. The Hyundai Accent has a smashed front bumper.
18. Phyllis O'Meara says she has noticed traffic on West Hill Road has been busier than usual for several days.
19. The weather is sunny.

The solution for this exercise can be found on this book's companion website at www.toserveandprotect.nelson.com.

In this chapter we have practised a number of foundational skills. As with all skills, continued practice is necessary, but the skills will continue to develop throughout an officer's career.

A Note on Listening Skills

Computer programmers have a saying: GIGO, meaning, "garbage in, garbage out." They mean that if the programmer hasn't gathered accurate, relevant, and useful information, the resulting program will be flawed, no matter how well written. In the same way, if an officer does not use good listening skills to gather information, his or her documentation will be useless or even harmful in the process of achieving justice. Here are just a few guidelines in terms of using your ears as well as your eyes in dealing with victims, witnesses, and suspects during an investigation:

- Focus: an incident or crime scene can be chaotic, and emotions can run high. Focus carefully on the person with whom you are speaking.
- Be aware of body language: Words carry only a small part of a person's message. Be careful with your body language, and at the same time pay attention to what you can learn from the body language of others. Experienced officers notice eye contact, perspiration, nervous tics (what a poker player calls a "tell"), and so on.
- Interrupt only if strategic: Most of us have a tendency to jump in and interrupt when someone else is talking. An experienced officer interrupts only when it is strategic to do so. Having listening skills means that you actually listen!
- Use silence: Nature abhors a vacuum. In North America, we tend to hate silence in a conversation, and rush to fill it up. This is not true of all cultures; aboriginal cultures, for example, often value silence as a sign of reflection and respect. For many others, though, silence is often uncomfortable, and an experienced officer can use silence on his or her part to elicit information from a reluctant interviewee.
- Ask clarifying questions: Get to precise details by asking follow-up questions (e.g., "You say the suspect

was tall. Was he about my height? A bit taller? How much shorter? Would he reach about my shoulder?" and so on).

- Paraphrase for understanding, and ask for paraphrasing to indicate understanding: Being able to put something in one's own words indicates an understanding of the message. The speaker can then confirm that what the listener understood is indeed what the speaker meant. Note that in a valid arrest, an officer is advised to have the person detained paraphrase the caution and right to counsel to confirm the detainee's understanding of these rights.

- Be culturally sensitive: As mentioned above regarding silence, different cultures have different norms and expectations regarding body language and other par- alinguistic features (personal space, loudness of the voice, and so on). For example, an officer related to me a story about investigating an assault. When he inter- viewed the young woman's family, they served him tea and smiled throughout the interview. Having had diversity training, he understood that this behaviour did not indicate a callous disregard for the daughter's ordeal, but a culturally appropriate way of interacting with a person of authority. Rather than indicating hap- piness, the smiling was a manifestation of the family's deep discomfort. It is essential that an officer be able to see beyond the norms of his or her background in order to listen to and understand others.

EXPLORATIONS

1.1 Look at a number of police websites, such as the following, to find descriptions of missing persons or suspects (when using the Saskatoon Police site, search "Request for Public Assistance):

www.peelpolice.on.ca/Crime%20Files/Peels%20Most% 20Wanted.aspx

www.police.saskatoon.sk.ca/index.php?loc=videos/ request.php

http://vancouver.ca/MissingPersons_wac/MissingPersons .exe

http://vancouver.ca/mostwanted_wac/mostwanted.exe

1.2 Select a photo of a person to describe. It can be a photo from a family album, one you find on Facebook, or one from a magazine. Describe the person in detail. Check out the newspapers in your area, especially community newspapers, for photos of accidents or crime scenes you can describe. Choose a photo and write a detailed description of the scene.

1.3. Go to the following websites and look at the paintings you find. Look at the details of the paintings in the way described in "Did You Notice Their Guns?" above. What do you see?

www.artchive.com/artchive/V/vermeer/missmaid.jpg.html

www.wga.hu/frames-e.html?/html/g/greco_el/14/1402grec .html

http://collections.frick.org/

1.4 Watch the movie *12 Angry Men*. Write a paragraph or short essay on the lessons this movie offers to someone going into law enforcement.

1.5 Discuss a current or classic movie. What can be learned from it by someone going into law enforcement?

1.6 Research an instance of a wrongful conviction (e.g., Stephen Truscott, Guy Paul Morin, David Milgaard). What may have led to the incorrect conclusion about the person's guilt?

1.7 View the last few pages of the document posted at www .torontopolice.on.ca/careers/oacpguide.pdf for another example of a scrambled occurrence. Write a narrative of several paragraphs in length that helps the reader see what happened.

1.8 Explore an ethnic or racial group in your community. What typical body language and other paralinguistic features should culturally sensitive officers be aware of? Many immigrants come from parts of the world where police are corrupt and/or the feared agents of a repressive government. What is this group's prior experience with police, either in their native country or here in Canada?

Solution to Five-Minute Mystery

A deaf person would not react to ambient [background] noise by raising her voice to compensate for it. Quite likely, Mrs. Van Nough can hear, and if so, would find it difficult to explain why she did not hear the gunshot that killed poor Alvin while she was supposedly on the porch.

Chapter 2

Context of Canadian Police Writing

The viewing public has an insatiable appetite for television shows and movies about law enforcement. Think of the cop shows you have seen. Think about the movies you've watched that have featured police or law enforcement officers. What were the key characteristics of the daily work portrayed? I'll bet it wasn't the endless paperwork to be completed each day. In reality, police officers write more during the course of their careers than almost any other profession, with the exception of lawyers and journalists. A police department's day is captured in writing.

> There is much required writing in the field of policing. It starts with a call for service, which is documented by a communications operator. Responding officers are then required to record information in a memo book and are routinely required to write witness statements. This information is required to be written into an occurrence or arrest report. This same information may be written into either arrest or search warrants and possibly into internal reports.

Some of this paperwork was always there, but there is no question that the need for documentation has increased in recent decades. For example, as a result of Supreme Court of Canada decisions based on the Charter of Rights and Freedoms, the Crown is required to provide full disclosure to the defence of all information relating to a case at the time of laying a charge; in the past, such information as was disclosed was shared only when a "not guilty" plea was entered. Since approximately 80 percent of cases in some jurisdictions are and were resolved through a guilty plea, in the past only 20 percent of charges resulted in disclosure; that number is now 100 percent (Ericson & Haggerty, 1997, p. 325). Other Supreme Court decisions have increased the requirement for paperwork connected with search warrants and arrest warrants. Please see the box below.

Selected Supreme Court of Canada Decisions

R. v. Stinchcombe:

Held that the Crown has a legal duty to disclose all relevant information to the defense. "The fruits of the investigation which are in its possession are not the property of the Crown for use in securing a conviction but the property of the public to be used to ensure that justice is done."

R. v. Feeney:

Held that police need prior judicial authorization of entry into a dwelling house in order to effect an arrest, except in exceptional ("exigent") circumstances. A new type of warrant, commonly called a Feeney warrant, was developed for this purpose.

R. v. Askov:

Held that an accused individual has the right to be tried within a reasonable time, which creates an urgency regarding documentation.

Source: Supreme Court of Canada and LexUM Laboratory of University of Montreal's Faculty of Law. *Supreme Court of Canada: Decisions.* Retrieved September 29, 2008, from http://scc.lexum.umontreal.ca.

Required documentation has led to many departments increasing the civilian member component of their service, in an effort to "keep cops on the street, instead of at the photocopier."

Nevertheless, the ever-increasing need for documentation remains a challenge, and an inescapable part of a law enforcement officer's life.

Table 2.1

NUMBER OF UNIFORM AND CIVILIAN MEMBERS
IN SELECTED CANADIAN POLICE DEPARTMENTS

Department	Number of Uniform Members	Number of Civilian Members
Calgary	1600+	855
Edmonton	1531	537
Montreal	4485	1046
Peel Region	1739	677
Toronto	5477	1807
Vancouver	1200+	300+

Source: The Calgary Police Service (www.calgarypolice.ca); The Edmonton Police Service (www.edmontonpolice.ca); Service de police de la Ville de Montréal (www.spvm.qc.ca); Peel Regional Police (www.peelpolice.ca); Toronto Police Service (www.torontopolice.on.ca); Vancouver Police Department (www.vancouver.ca/police).

Before looking at the uses of such documentation, we will take a look at the philosophy behind Canadian policing and the roles of a police officer.

The Roles of a Police Officer: Peel's Principles

Modern policing has its roots in the work of Robert Peel, the British Home Secretary who in 1829 established the London Metropolitan Police. As you pursue a career in law enforcement, you will be exposed many times to "Peel's Principles"; it is worth looking closely at these principles to see what they have to say about the reality of effective policing in a democracy. Policing is quite different in a democracy than in a "police state," a totalitarian regime where there are few or no checks on government and police actions. A democracy is government by the will of the people, and effective policing in a democracy is based on working with the people, not against them. Peel's Principles are grounded in this fundamental truth.

Context of Canadian Police Writing

Peel set forth nine principles. The first concerns the role of police, which is to *prevent* crime and disorder. He did not see the primary role of police as dealing with crime after the fact; rather, effective policing would stop crime before it occurred. For an analogy, think of our current approach to health services; effective medical care prevents disease, rather than merely being concerned with curing it. In the same way, according to Peel, effective policing is proactive rather than reactive, focusing on preventing criminal incidents rather than its main function being to round up the usual suspects.

Peel's other principles flow from this basic premise. Principle two states that police ability to carry out their role is dependent on the public's approval of their actions; a corollary to this (principle three) is that police need to obtain the willing cooperation of the public in voluntary observation of the law. Think about the implications of this, and how insightful Peel was. Police can only be effective if the vast majority of citizens voluntarily observe the laws of the land. (Otherwise, how many jails can we possibly build?) Democracy is a social contract. As citizens we have rights and responsibilities. While there may be a bit of larceny in everyone's soul, the vast majority of people will comply with the Criminal Code without even thinking about it.

However, the degree of cooperation with the police, according to Peel, is in inverse relation to the police use of force. In the same way, public favour and approval is gained and kept by the police being impartial, showing neither favouritism nor bias (principles four and five). According to Peel, force should be used only when all other means fail (principle six). In most policing organizations today there is mandatory annual training on use of force, and required written justification whenever force, especially lethal force, is used.

Principle number seven is the one most often quoted today. Peel made it clear that the police and the people were not separate or different—us against them. In fact, every citizen has a duty to maintain order; the police are simply members of the public who are paid to give full-time attention to that common duty. The implication of this is that there is and should be no divide between police and public.

Principle number eight deals with the legitimate role of police. The police are not the judiciary. A police officer is the gatherer of facts; a judge or jury is the trier of facts. The police gather evidence that provide reasonable grounds to lay a charge; a judge or jury determines guilt. The implications of this role differentiation for police writing will be discussed in detail in subsequent chapters, but in brief, police writing is objective, detailed, and impartial. The facts of a case are presented, as clearly as they are known, so that a judge or jury can make an informed decision about the guilt or innocence of a suspect.

Peel's ninth principle goes back full circle to his foundational first premise. According to Peel, the test of police efficiency is the absence of crime and disorder, not the visible evidence of police actions in dealing with crime and disorder. Again, the primary role for police is not the successful investigation of crime, but crime prevention. As we will see below, successful crime prevention in modern policing is underpinned by clear precise writing on the front lines; strategic community policing is grounded in data recorded throughout an officer's day.

The Roles of a Police Officer: Modern Day

An example of modern-day thinking of the roles of police can be found in Ontario's Police Services Act.

Ontario Police Services Act, Section 42

```
42. (1) The duties of a police officer include,
        (a) preserving the peace;
        (b) preventing crimes and other offences and
            providing assistance and encouragement
            to other persons in their prevention;
        (c) assisting victims of crime;
        (d) apprehending   criminals   and   other
            offenders and others who may lawfully be
            taken into custody;
```

(e) laying charges and participating in prosecutions;

(f) executing warrants that are to be executed by police officers and performing related duties;

(g) performing the lawful duties that the chief of police assigns;

(h) in the case of a municipal police force and in the case of an agreement under section 10 (agreement for provision of police services by O.P.P.), enforcing municipal by-laws;

(i) completing the prescribed training.

Source: *Police Services Act, Revised Statutes of Ontario 1990.* Copyright © Queen's Printer for Ontario.

Notice that the first two duties are preventative: preserving the peace, preventing crime, and helping and encouraging others (presumably non-police) to prevent crime. The third focuses on victim assistance. The fourth, fifth, and sixth duties concern crime investigation, suspect apprehension, and supporting the judicial process. All these duties are dependent in some way on effective writing.

Uses of Police Writing

As stated above, a police department's day is captured in writing. From the operator in the Communications Centre documenting, prioritizing, and dealing with calls for service, to the constable on patrol capturing relevant details in his notebook and in required reports, to the detective working with a patrol officer's initial report and adding supplementary reports throughout an investigation, to the criminal intelligence analyst sifting through data and crunching the numbers to provide a basis for strategic decision making, to the sergeant sharing information and communicating policy changes with her platoon, to the inspector writing a business case, to the senior command developing strategic plans, to the chief of police presenting a report to the Police Services Board—the day is filled with writing that helps to accomplish the department's mission.

Police writing is used in many ways. These uses can be broken into five categories:

- Occurrence investigation
- Criminal justice process
- Incident/Crime analysis
- Public relations
- Securing and maintaining financial support

Occurrence Investigation

The data collected in writing in an officer's notebook (memorandum book) is crucial in the successful investigation and resolution of an occurrence. An officer concentrates on collecting significant details; in fact, as we shall see in the next chapter, it can be said that officers as a group tend to over-record, just in case a seemingly irrelevant detail proves to be significant as the investigation continues. Information in the memorandum book forms the basis for all subsequent reports. Cases are sometimes handed over to other patrol officers or to detectives from the Criminal Investigation Branch or special units. Those officers rely on the original documentation to ground their subsequent investigation. Substantial rework and loss of time could result if these officers have to repeat steps of the original investigation because of sketchy or confusing documentation.

As well, data from reports is entered into databases that can be accessed by law enforcement personnel within the policing organization or even across the country. In addition to creating their local databases, policing services from across the country are required to provide criminal case statistics to Statistics Canada for the Uniform Crime Reporting (UCR) survey. (See the box below for an explanation of how this information, all of which is grounded on those original notebook entries, is used.)

Uniform Crime Reporting Survey

The Canadian Centre for Justice Statistics (CCJS), in co-operation with the policing community, collects police-reported crime statistics through the Uniform Crime Reporting Survey (UCR). The UCR Survey was designed to measure the incidence of crime in Canadian society and its characteristics.

UCR data reflect reported crime that has been substantiated by police. Information collected by the survey includes the number of criminal incidents, the clearance status of those incidents and persons-charged information. The UCR Survey produces a continuous historical record of crime and traffic statistics reported by every police agency in Canada since 1962. In 1988, a new version of the survey was created, UCR2, and is since referred to as the "incident-based" survey, in which microdata on characteristics of incidents, victims and accused are captured.

Data from the UCR Survey provide key information for crime analysis, resource planning and program development for the policing community. Municipal and provincial governments use the data to aid decisions about the distribution of police resources, definitions of provincial standards and for comparisons with other departments and provinces.

To the federal government, the UCR survey provides information for policy and legislative development, evaluation of new legislative initiatives, and international comparisons.

To the public, the UCR survey offers information on the nature and extent of police-reported crime and crime trends in Canada. As well, media, academics and researchers use these data to examine specific issues about crime.

Source: Extract from Statistics Canada, *Uniform Crime Reporting Survey, 2007*, http://www.statcan.ca/cgi-bin/imdb/p2SV.pl?Function=getSurvey&SDDS=3302&lang=en&db=IMDB&dbg=f&adm=8&dis=2, accessed August 2008.

Criminal Justice Process

Police documents play a crucial role in the criminal justice process. Justices of the peace evaluate written requests for search warrants or arrest warrants before granting or denying these requests. Crown attorneys rely on documentation from police, most specifically the Crown Brief, in deciding on a course of action in regard to an individual case, for example, whether to prosecute and whether to offer a plea bargain. As mentioned above, as a result of *R. v. Stinchcombe*, full disclosure to the defence of the documentation relating to a case is required when charges are filed, which has led to a substantial increase in the volume of police writing.

With respect to *Stinchcombe*, the difference between where we were and where we are now arises from the fact that we provide information to the crown in preparation for a court case. We generally didn't do so until the accused had made their first appearance and had entered a not guilty plea. If they made their first appearance and pleaded guilty, there was a short arrest report completed at the time of the arrest which was a sort of overview of the charges and gave the crown prosecutor something to relate to the court, the nature of the offense, which the accused or his representatives would either agree to or make some sort of addendum to. Then the judge would deal with it from there. *Stinchcombe* has caused us to do . . . what we used to do when we received a not guilty plea, which was a more elaborate court presentation outlining in greater detail what every witness would contribute to the prosecution and, in addition, a greater burden to provide information that the prosecution may not call but could be deemed as relevant to the defence's side of the process. And the significant difference is that now we have to do that prior to the indication of plea . . .

Source: From Ericson, R.V., and K.D. Haggerty. (1997). *Policing the Risk Society*, p. 325. Toronto: University of Toronto Press.

Any deficiencies in the written record can undermine a successful prosecution. (And, remember, while the Crown must fully disclose its case, the defence has no such requirement. If deemed strategic, a defence attorney could wait until an officer is on the stand to pounce publicly and quite embarrassingly on the flaws in an officer's paperwork.)

Another role for police documentation in the justice system is to provide an invaluable aid to memory before testimony at trial. Detailed notebooks and precise, clear witness statements are essential. Witnesses are allowed to reread their signed statements before giving evidence in a trial, since the courts recognize that memory is dimmed through the passage of time, but can be refreshed. Detailed witness statements are crucial to allow witnesses that process of re-remembering.

Incident/Crime Analysis

To fulfill their mandate to prevent crime, police organizations engage in strategic, intelligence-led policing. Many services have dedicated criminal intelligence analysts who mine the data gathered in various police reports. The results of their analysis can be used by the organization in many ways. For instance, unit commanders can determine the best allocation of patrol resources, setting up targeted patrols in certain areas and at designated times. For example, data reveals that the entertainment district in Toronto is subject to disorder on weekends during certain peak periods in the late evening and early morning. Criminal incidents can be curtailed by officer presence and proactive police strategies. Additional foot and bicycle patrols can be scheduled for those times.

In the same way, crime analysis data can provide the basis for decisions as to the best location for community police stations. My neighbourhood originally had a community police station that was adjacent to a playground, baseball diamond, community centre, and soccer field. Data showed that the area had very little crime, while a busy street location about six kilometres away was experiencing an increase in criminal activity. The community station was moved; the former station is now used as a property unit. Not only did crime analysis data allow the decision to be made, but sharing of that data also addressed neighbourhood concerns at the loss of the station.

Data mining can also alert organizations to subtle changes in an area that could potentially lead to more serious policing issues. Through capturing "quality of life" offences, such as graffiti and other vandalism, services can practise preventative policing in areas that are not yet crime-prone to keep them from becoming so. This preventative policing is based on the "broken window" theory. According to this theory, a broken window in a building that remains unrepaired invites others to break the rest of the windows. Not addressing quality-of-life issues, according to this theory, leads to resident fear, subsequent avoidance of public space, and ultimately more serious crime and disorder.

Crime analysis also can help a service help the public to protect itself. For example, at a recent community policing open house meeting in the west end of Toronto, attended by approximately 100 residents, those in attendance were alerted to a trend concerning the theft of high-end vehicles. Such vehicles cannot be hot-wired, but require the car's specific key. Therefore, while most burglaries usually take place during the day while many people are at work, thieves wishing to steal these luxury vehicles were breaking into houses while residents were home in order to steal the keys, usually hanging on a hook by the door, and then stealing the vehicle—a much more risky undertaking for both victim and criminal. Interestingly, many of the houses targeted had alarm systems, but occupants did not activate those systems while they were in the house but still awake (i.e., they usually turned them on when they turned off the lights and went to bed).

Other organizations also use crime analysis data. For example, data concerning traffic collisions is used by legislators seeking to set a safe speed limit, or by insurance agencies in settling claims.

Most policing organizations conduct environmental scans to predict trends for various types of crime. Check out the website of the police service in your area for an environmental scan. If your local service doesn't publish that report, look at the one you'll find at this website: www.torontopoliceservice/publications/files/reports/2006envscan.pdf.

In what ways is the environmental scan rooted in the work of individual patrol officers and the writing they do?

Data mining is useful no matter what the size of a police service. For instance, the Saskatoon Police Service, with 398 uniform and 107 civilian members, introduced CompStat in 2007, which allowed them to "direct resources to emerging crime trends." Their chief of police reports a resulting 9.6 percent reduction in property crime, and a 26 percent reduction in break and enters (www.police.saskatoon.sk.ca).

Public Relations

Recall that Peel said that police are dependent on public approval to be effective in carrying out their tasks. One use of police data is in garnering that public support. The community meeting mentioned above is one example of public relations. A good deal of data was shared throughout the meeting. The data was a concrete demonstration of the officers' competence, professionalism, and dedication.

Annual reports published by police services accomplish the same objective. Go to your local service's website and locate the annual report. How is it different from the environmental scan? An annual report is a "feel good" document. It is often glitzy, loaded with photographs and human interest material. While dependent on data, an annual report is less data-heavy than an environmental scan. An environmental scan is a more in-depth analysis of crime statistics and demographic trends; an annual report skims the surface to assure citizens that the enterprise is in order.

On a more regular basis throughout the year, departments will issue press releases. Sometimes these are for public relations, and sometimes are issued as an aid to an investigation, asking for the public's help in solving a case. These press releases are sent to the media and posted on the home page of department websites. Older press releases are often archived on the site as well. When posted on a department's website, the releases involve more than words alone and include pictures and even video clips. Check out the home pages of various police departments to get a sense of what a press release from a police service looks like.

Securing and Maintaining Financial Support

Police services are public service organizations. They rely on governments for their budgets. In municipalities with their own police service, or in parts of the country with regional police services, policing accounts for a very large portion of a municipality or region's annual budget. Governments want value for their dollar; data help to demonstrate the value achieved. However, consider Peel's ninth principle. If the test of police efficiency is the absence of crime and disorder, not the visible evidence of police actions in dealing with crime and disorder, then how can that efficiency (value for the dollar) be demonstrated in concrete data?

Policing organizations set standards of performance, for example, desired response times to calls, and gather and often publish data capturing that performance. Interpretation of that data, though, is problematic. Is a shortfall in achieving a given performance standard caused by department inefficiency or by understaffing? Writing again comes into play as these data are analyzed and used as the basis for change or for requests for more resources.

This has been a brief introduction to the context in which police writing takes place. Keep these contexts in mind as you read the next chapters.

EXPLORATIONS

2.1 Visit the police website in your community as well as other police websites. Look at the message from the chief of police or chief constable. Explore the website. What can you learn about the vision, mission, and values of these departments, as well as the issues they face?

2.2 Newspapers frequently report on crime in a community, as well as on court cases. Spend some time looking at area newspapers to get a sense of the context for policing in your community.

2.3 Trials are usually open to the public. Attend a court session and note the use of police documentation in the judicial process.

2.4 As mentioned in this chapter, civilian members are an important portion of a policing service. Explore civilian roles in your community's police department. What opportunities exist for non-uniform members to make a contribution?

References

Ericson, R. V., & K. D. Haggerty. (1997). *Policing the risk society.* Toronto: University of Toronto Press.

Chapter 3

Police Memorandum Books (Notebooks)

On March 9, 1988, John Joseph Harper was shot and killed by a Winnipeg police officer. Harper had been stopped on suspicion of stealing a car; it was later shown that he did not fully fit the description of the suspect. Harper had been walking home after a night of drinking; when asked for identification, he would not cooperate. An altercation occurred with the officer; in the scuffle, Harper was fatally wounded. The officer would claim that he thought Harper was grabbing for the officer's gun, and the gun discharged.

At first the matter was handled internally by the police department. After a brief investigation, the officer was deemed to be acting in self-defence. The ensuing public outcry led to a provincial inquiry. Among other findings, the Report of the Aboriginal Justice Inquiry of Manitoba had much to say about the notebooks of the officers who were on duty that night. Memo books were not promptly and properly completed. Notes made on scratch paper were lost and then reconstructed. Officers appeared to have colluded to ensure they "had their stories straight." One officer rewrote his entire notebook, changing details and using the rewritten memo book as the source of initial testimony before the inquiry. The inquiry recommended incorporating notebook management practices from other jurisdictions and enhancing notebook training to ensure that the accuracy of memo books would not be in question, since they are so crucial. (See www.ajic.mb.ca for a recounting of the incident and subsequent recommendations regarding many areas of police procedure in this case).

An officer's notebook, also referred to as a memorandum or memo book, is a record of every significant incident that takes place during an officer's shift. The officer records the time he or she reported for duty, details of the weather and road conditions, significant facts from briefing (called "parade" in some services), all in-service times, and the times and details of all activities. A memo book is the log of a shift. As we saw in the last chapter, it is used to provide details that could lead to the resolution of an incident, as well as to refresh an officer's memory for court appearances. Information in the memorandum book provides the basis for subsequent reports and data collection. Accurate, detailed notebooks are essential for successful clearance of occurrences. Officers tend to record any details that might prove useful in the future, deliberately over-recording (Ericson & Haggerty, 1997, p. 325). One of my students, a veteran officer, shared that memorandum books are becoming increasingly more detailed, since the implication given by defence attorneys in court is that "if it isn't in the memo book, it didn't happen."

In some provinces, such as Ontario, the accountability provided by memo books is considered so important that all sworn members of a police service, including the chief of police, are required by law to keep a notebook. Notebooks are not an instance of collaborative writing; each officer attending a scene records his or her notes in the memo book without collusion. Notebooks are the property of the police service, not the individual officer, and care is taken to provide for the notebook's integrity.

It is essential for a police service to maintain the public's trust, and to remain above suspicion. Detailed procedures for the keeping of an officer's notebook are drawn up by police services to maintain the integrity of these crucial records. Training in these procedures is a part of pre-service education. There may be minor differences in those procedures among various police services; this chapter deals with their fundamentals.

Before we begin, think for one minute. If you wanted to ensure the integrity of notebooks, and therefore public trust in their content, what would you do? What guidelines would you set? What safeguards would you put in place? For example, what would the notebook look like?

Notebook entries are made throughout a shift, so the notebook must be portable as it must always be with an officer. To demonstrate the integrity of its content, a memo book should be bound, rather than having pages that can be easily torn out or lost. To enhance credibility, pages should be numbered to demonstrate without a doubt that no pages are missing. To help locate the exact memo book dealing with a certain shift (since officers will complete many memo books in a year), the cover should include a space for the date of the first and last entry (e.g., Period covered by notebook: June 1, 2008–June 12, 2008). There should be a place to record an officer's name, rank, and badge number.

All entries in the notebook should be made in permanent (not erasable) ink. Black ink is preferred in order to facilitate photocopying if needed. No lines should be skipped, except between days worked, to ensure that nothing could be or has been added to the memo book at a later time. If a mistake is made, errors should not be scratched out, rendering them indecipherable ("Constable, what are you trying to hide?"). Instead, errors should be crossed out with a single line and then initialled. Some services even require that officers draw a line from their last word written out to the edge of the paper, to ensure and make clear that nothing has been added after the fact. See Table 3.1, below, for an example of this

Table 3.1

SAMPLE NOTEBOOK ENTRY

	Thursday, June 26, 2008
	0:700–15:00
06:45	Report for duty
	Weather: light rain, overcast
	Roads: slick
07:00	Briefing conducted Sgt. WALSH
	Missing person: Fred SMITH, 78 (DOB Feb. 7, 1930) Caucasian, 5 ft. 8 in., 156 lbs., bald, wearing grey-striped pyjamas, no teeth (dentures), missing from 14 Pine Crescent, dementia
07:15	In-service, general patrol

practice; the other examples of notebooks do not contain this feature.

The recording of each shift should begin with the day of the week and date (including year) of the shift, followed by scheduled hours of work. An officer should note the time she or he reported for duty, and list the weather and road conditions. Why would this information be recorded? When might the recording of weather and road conditions prove useful or relevant?

To avoid confusion, police services usually use a twenty-four-hour clock (military or railroad time). If you are unfamiliar with the twenty-four-hour system, please see Table 3.2, below. Whether or not to include the colon in the time in the twenty-four-hour service (12:15 instead of 1215) appears to be a matter of convention. We have included the colon in all

Table 3.2

COMPARISON OF STANDARD AND TWENTY-FOUR-HOUR CLOCK

Standard Clock	Twenty-Four-Hour Clock
1:00 a.m.	01:00
2:00 a.m.	02:00
3:00 a.m.	03:00
4:00 a.m.	04:00
5:00 a.m.	05:00
6:00 a.m.	06:00
7:00 a.m.	07:00
8:00 a.m.	08:00
9:00 a.m.	09:00
10:00 a.m.	10:00
11:00 a.m.	11:00
Noon	12:00
1:00 p.m.	13:00
2:00 p.m.	14:00
3:00 p.m.	15:00
4:00 p.m.	16:00
5:00 p.m.	17:00
6:00 p.m.	18:00
7:00 p.m.	19:00
8:00 p.m.	20:00
9:00 p.m.	21:00
10:00 p.m.	22:00
11:00 p.m.	23:00
Midnight	24:00

examples. Follow the practice recommended by your teacher (and later, by your coach officer).

Notebooks can be written in point form, so long as there is no possibility of misinterpretation. An entry that causes an officer to scratch his or her head months later—"What on earth did I mean by that?"—or that is ambiguous is worse than useless.

The memo book should record precise details. As stated, it will be used as the basis for all subsequent reports, so care must be taken that all needed information is captured in this initial data-gathering. The language of the notebook should be clear and factual. The officer should describe what was observed by himself or herself and by witnesses. Sensory data should be captured: What was seen? Heard? Smelled? Even the other two senses (taste and touch) might come into play in certain incidents. An officer's task is to recreate the occurrence for himself or herself so that it can be understood and to enable the recreation of an occurrence so that another person can vicariously experience it. Careful attention to sensory details will facilitate these recreations. See below for an example.

Table 3.3

NOTEBOOK ENTRY RECREATING AN OCCURRENCE

14:00	Dispatched to 106 Carter Rd, possible missing or injured person.
	Met by Cheryl MILLER, 104 Carter Road, 416-773-5592
	MILLER had not seen neighbour at 106 Carter Rd for two days.
	Elma LANCASTER, approx. 80 years old, approx. 5 ft. tall, 130 lb.
	Widow; 2 children out of province, no other family.
	Good health, frequently confused. 106 Carter Rd. is narrow 2-story house.
	Knocked and called at front door. Negative. Went to back door. Strong smell on porch of rotting meat. Knocked and called at back door. Negative. Pushed in door.
	Kitchen at back of house. Spoiled food on table and on dishes in sink. Newspapers and store flyers on all chairs and in several piles on floor. Strong urine smell from cat litter box along wall near door to next room. Empty cat feeding dish.
	Could hear cat meowing. Living room at front of the house. Dim light. Heavy curtains pulled shut. Dishevelled room—papers, bags, boxes on all surfaces. Stairs in corner leading to upstairs. Found Elma LANCASTER crumpled at base of stairs.
	Called her name. LANCASTER opened eyes, asked if her father was home.
	Took vitals. Called ambulance. ? broken leg. ? dehydration.
14:20	Ambulance arrived. LANCASTER transported to Sherway General Hospital for assessment and ? Social Service intervention.

The notebook should account for the officer's time. If an officer is not attending to a specific duty or on break, the time is listed as in service or general patrol. An officer on general patrol is available for dispatch. To facilitate recording, many police services use 10-codes as shorthand for various activities. These codes may vary among different services, and are generally printed in a reference section at the back of the notebook, or on the back cover. Some common 10-codes are 10-8 (in service on general patrol), 10-7 (out of service), and 10-43 (on lunch). Some departments discourage or prohibit the use of 10-codes because of the variations in meaning and the consequent potential for misunderstanding and confusion.

Memorandum books will often also include the exact wording of the caution, right to counsel, and right to a 24-hour legal hotline that must be read to someone who is arrested or detained (an alternative is a separate card carried by officers). If someone is arrested or detained, an officer must read these instructions to the suspect, record in the notebook that they were read, ask the suspect if she or he understood the rights, and record the exact words of the suspect that demonstrate understanding. Please see Table 3.4 for an example.

While conversations with complainants and witnesses can be paraphrased, conversations with suspects or accused persons must be captured in the notebook verbatim (word-for-word). These conversations are generally captured as though they were dialogue in a play, with the initials of each speaker in the notebook margin, and the words of each speaker given exactly. As in the text for a play, body language is also noted (shrugged,

Table 3.4

NOTEBOOK ENTRY TO RECORD THE READING OF RIGHTS

	I read the suspect the right to counsel and caution from my memo book.
L.V.	Do you understand these rights as I have read them to you?
J.S.	Yeah, I get it. I didn't do nothing, so I don't need a lawyer. Ask me what you want. I got nothing to hide.

pointed middle finger and spat, etc.). Silence or lack of response is also noted. Please see the example below.

Table 3.5

VERBATIM NOTEBOOK ENTRY

L.V.	According to a witness, you were seen with a baseball bat at five minutes past midnight in the parking lot where your boyfriend's car was parked.
J.S.	(shrugs) So? I'm on a softball team. Besides, I had nothing else to do, since that bastard stood me up to go drinking with his buddies (pounds right fist into left hand and shakes head from side to side). My mother was right about him.
L.V.	Did you smash your boyfriend's windshield with the bat?
J.S.	(No response.) (Looks at floor.)

Capturing conversation verbatim is a difficult skill. Your teacher may choose to show your class "Mary's Arrest," a clip on the text website that recreates an arrest, or ask you to view it on your own. Try to capture the conversation between the officer and Mary. What makes it difficult to record the conversation verbatim?

Information in the memorandum book is used to provide justification for an officer's actions, including alternative resolutions other than arrest. Remember Peel's principle concerning impartiality. In recent years, questions have been raised concerning officers' use of discretion. Concerns have sometimes been expressed that officers may show bias in terms of who is charged and who is dealt with by alternative means. Officers can be called to account for their use of discretion in this area. The information captured in the notebook should provide a sound basis for any decision by an officer.

At the end of a shift, the officer records off-duty time and signs the notebook, taking ownership thereby of its contents. In many services, the officer's supervisor also signs the memo book, thus taking accountability for its integrity on behalf of the organization. Please see the example below.

Table 3.6

NOTEBOOK SIGN-OFF

15:00	Off-Duty
	Cst. *Luke Vader*, #3241
	Sgt. *Pat Willis*, #2213
	Friday, June 29
	07:00–15:00

In many departments, officers also record off-duty, sick days, and vacation days in their notebook, so that an officer's entire year is accounted for.

Consider for a moment the environment in which an officer does his or her writing. Picture an officer recording the events of a shift in the memo book. Here's what some practising officers have said about their writing environment:

> Writing [in typical police circumstances] . . . is both a physical and mental challenge. There are few other occupations in which a writer has to face the particular challenges frequently encountered in policing.

> The writing is routinely conducted in a busy work environment, with other distractions. Sometimes writing is done when fatigue and stress is present, which can have an impact.

Focusing on the potential uses of the writing, as discussed in Chapter 2, and the tremendous importance of doing it well can help an officer deal with the physical and mental challenge of the task.

Supporting Materials for This Chapter

The following two pages provide a criteria sheet for evaluating notebooks. Your teacher may choose to use this criteria sheet for a notebook assignment, or may choose to modify it for your circumstances. The criteria sheet is followed by an abridged sample of a complete shift, explorations, and a few possible incidents you might use as raw material for a notebook or report assignment.

Table 3.7

CRITERIA SHEET FOR NOTEBOOK EVALUATION

	Fail	Minimum Pass	Solid Pass	Pass with Excellence
FORMAT				
• written on every line				
• errors are readable				
• tasks recorded chronologically				
• title for each day (day, date)				
• scheduled hours of work				
• time reported for duty				
• road and weather conditions				
• twenty-four-hour system used				
• briefing time and relevant info				
• initial in-service time recorded				
• time of each task recorded				
• off-duty time recorded				
• notebook signed				
CONTENT				
• info recorded that would be needed for General Occurrence Report/Arrest report cover page				
• use of precise, concrete details				
• inclusion of factors affecting observations				
• verbatim conversation recorded appropriately				

Table 3.8

EXAMPLE OF A NOTEBOOK FOR ONE FULL SHIFT

	Friday, August 1, 2008
	15:00–01:00
14:30	Report for duty
	Weather: sunny, muggy.
	Roads: dry.
15:00	Briefing conducted by Sgt. BOCELLI.
	Several high-end auto thefts in Baycrest area; M_
	when owners are home; no suspects.
15:15	In service; general patrol

Police Memorandu

Table 3.8 (continued)

16:30	Mason Drive at Berrydale Parkette
	7–8 males, ages approx. 12 years old, clustered in circle, shouting.
	Stop cruiser to investigate; 3 boys run west on Mason Drive.
	Remaining 4 boys move aside; on ground are two boys wrestling and punching each other.
	I tell them to stop fighting and stand up; direct other boys to disperse.
	James FLANAGAN DOB April 2, 1996
	4453 Monks Lane 416-664-7723
	Bleeding nose, developing bruises on right arm, torn teeshirt.
	Fred PARADIS DOB June 4, 1996
	395 Clark Road 416-523-8491
	Developing black eye, bruised knuckles, torn knee on shorts.
	Discussed situation with boys; they shook hands and were sent home.
16:50	In-service; general patrol
19:00	Lunch break; out of service
19:45	In service; general patrol
20:15	As cruiser came within 50 yards of Dowling St. and Serpa Way, saw silver 1998 four-door Cavalier Ontario tag OHL125 run red light. Engaged roof lights and siren. Cavalier pulled to side of road.
	Driver: Andrew Wilson DOB Jan. 2, 1985
	DL xxxxxxxxxxxxxxxxxxxxxxxx
	No priors; ticket issued.
20:30	In service; general patrol
21:00	Radio dispatch to 7 Tawny Lane, vehicle theft.
	Stolen: 2007 Porsche Carrera, cinnamon (medium brown) with dark brown leather seats.
	Ontario tag HALS TOY VIN 333333333333333
	Owner of car: Harold AIRD DOB May 14, 1953
	7 Tawny Lane 416-444-8876
	AIRD returned from work (Aird Financial Consulting, 233 Bay Street, 416-222-8888) at 19:00. AIRD and wife (Sheila AIRD, DOB October 10, 1963) ate dinner on patio at rear of house (2-storey, 2500 square foot, detached garage, 2 car driveway, patio and swimming pool at rear of house). Tawny Lane is a cul-de-sac with 5 houses. 7 Tawny Lane is third house. Driveway is not visible from rear of house.
	Car was discovered missing at 8:45. Sheila AIRD went out to car to bring in package from trunk. Side door of house jimmied; slight damage to door jamb.
	Keys missing from hook in kitchen near side door.
	Crime scene analysts called for possible prints.
	Canvassed rest of houses on street for witnesses. Negative results.
	Cst. *Alice Farrell*
	Sgt. *Paul Green*
	Saturday, August 2, 2008
	Off-duty

Off-duty time (01:00)

EXPLORATIONS

3.1 Look at the recommendations concerning police notebooks found in the conclusions of an inquiry into the wrongful conviction of Guy Paul Morin at located at www.attorney-general.jus.gov.on.ca/english/about/pubs/morin/morin_recom.pdf. How do they relate to the message of this chapter?

3.2 Record the notebook pages for a single shift, including three incidents. If you wish, you can take the incidents from the scenarios at the end of these Explorations (p. 68), from newspaper accounts of events, or you can generate them yourself. Follow the criteria sheet in this chapter or as modified by your teacher.

3.3 Peer review: Exchange the notebook pages created in Exploration 3.2 with a classmate. Pretend you are the supervisor of the officer who completed the notebook. Sign off the notebook after giving any feedback needed for improvement.

3.4 In pairs, complete the verbatim interview exercise below. (Alternatively, this can be done as individual homework by interviewing a friend or family member.)

Verbatim Interview of a Classmate

Interviewer: _____

Person Interviewed: _____

As the interviewer, assume that a crime was committed last night between 7:00 and 9:00 p.m.
Interview a classmate as to his or her whereabouts
last night between those times. Record your questions and the interviewee's responses verbatim. Then
switch roles.

The following conversation occurred:

_____

_____

_____

_____

_____

_____

_____

_____

_____

Incident Scenarios

Use the scenarios below as the basis for notebook entries or for reports. The scenarios are only a starting point; you need to create detailed information.

Traffic-Related

1. Your dispatcher sends you to a highway in your city. An elderly man has entered the off-ramp, and is driving slowly against the flow of traffic. When you stop him, he is confused and disoriented.

2. You are dispatched to a busy intersection. There you find a two-car collision. One car was travelling extremely fast, ran a red light, and hit another car that was about to enter the intersection. The second car slammed into a building on the corner and burst into flames. The driver will be taken to hospital with critical injuries. The driver of the first car is under the influence, and has only minor injuries.

3. You are dispatched to an intersection on the outskirts of your city or town. The speed limit is 80 km an hour on that stretch of road. A car was sitting at a stop light when it was hit from behind by another vehicle. The driver of the second vehicle is a young mother who was distracted by her baby crying in the car seat in the backseat of her car. She did not see the red light until right before impact; she hit the first car at 80 km per hour. Although injuries are relatively minor, both cars are severely damaged.

4. You are dispatched to a highway off-ramp. A young man did not decelerate when leaving the highway, and lost control of his vehicle as he exited.

5. You are dispatched to an intersection. There has been a two-car collision. One driver was making a left turn during an amber light, while another driver accelerated to cross the intersection before the light turned red. The turning driver was broadsided, and will be pronounced dead at the scene.

Disturbances

1. You are dispatched to a local bar. It is Karaoke Night. Two patrons are fighting. The first made fun of the second patron's girlfriend as she performed.

2. You are dispatched to a single family dwelling. The occupant claims his neighbour has threatened to kill the occupant's dog because the dog, who is housed in the back yard, barks constantly. The neighbour allegedly has thrown rocks at the dog.

3. You are dispatched to a single family dwelling. The occupant has been trimming a tree. The tree is in the backyard of the house behind him, but the branches extend into his yard. Standing on a ladder, he was trimming the branches on his side of the fence when the occupant of the house behind him, an older female, came out of the house and yelled at him to stop. Police were called when she began to shake the ladder, trying to knock down the ladder along with the person trimming the branches.

4. You are dispatched to a small six-apartment building because one resident hears a woman screaming in another apartment.

5. You are dispatched to a single family dwelling. You are met by a man who is quite upset. He claims that his girlfriend, with whom he still shares living space although the relationship has ended, has deliberately backed into his vehicle, an older model sports car. He was parked behind her in the driveway, blocking her in. She had asked him to move his car, since she was late for work. When he did not do so immediately, she allegedly got in her car and backed into his.

Break and Enter/Vandalism/Other

1. You are dispatched to a small street with fourteen houses on each side of the street. You find that all cars that were parked in the driveways or on the street have had their tires slashed.

2. You are dispatched to a single family dwelling to investigate a complaint of break and enter. On arrival, you find the complainant, an eighty-five-year-old woman, who accuses her next-door neighbours of entering the house through the side windows and stealing her possessions.

3. You are dispatched to a single family dwelling. The property is surrounded by a three-foot-high faux marble wall. One section of the wall has been spray painted with graffiti.

4. You are patrolling a city park. You see a group of underage teenage boys drinking in the park. There appear to be several cases of beer where they are sitting. As you approach, most of the boys run away, but two who stay tell you that their lacrosse team won the provincial championship that afternoon, and that is why they are celebrating.

5. You are dispatched to a single family dwelling. The female resident, a night-school teacher, is concerned because a man is parked in a car outside her house. He appears to be a student who was dissatisfied with his grade. The student has left threatening messages for her. Upon investigating, you discover that the male had actually been attending the class in place of his wife. The wife has a name that could identify either a male or female.

6. You are dispatched to a single family dwelling. The family reports that their elderly parent, who suffers from dementia, is missing.

References

Ericson, R. V., and Haggerty, K. D. (1997). *Policing the risk society*. Toronto: University of Toronto Press.

Chapter 4

Incident Reports, Arrest Reports, and Witness Statements

In this chapter we will cover two types of reports—incident reports and arrest reports—as well as the basics of witness statements. Incident reports, arrest reports, search warrants, arrest warrants—all are grounded in the original notetaking in an officer's memo book.

Most police reports today are created electronically. Technology allows for speedier entry of data, and reduces duplication of effort. As well, data collection and analysis are facilitated through electronic reporting. The reports in this chapter were created and filled out by the author in a common electronic reporting program. The basic form is found in Figure 4.1. The form is an example only, illustrating common features. Policing services create their own in-house forms or contract a forms service to develop these reporting tools.

Police reporting forms are typically multi-functional; for example, the same form is often used to report an incident and an arrest. One form is designed to cover many situations, with an officer identifying its purpose and deciding which sections to complete based on the situation.

Figure 4.1

SAMPLE REPORT FORM

Police Service Online Report Form

Report Type:

Incident Number

❏ General Occurrence Report
❏ Arrest Report
❏ Summons

Officer, Badge Number

Date and Time of Incident

Incident Location

Weapon ❏ No ❏ Yes ❏ Unknown

Type

Victim/Complainant

Last name   First   Middle   Maiden

Address

Home phone

Email address

Gender
❏ Male   ❏ Female

Date of Birth (Month/day/year)

Marital status
❏ Single ❏ Married ❏ Common-law ❏ Widowed ❏ Divorced

Employer

Work phone

(continued)

Work address

Condition ❐ Sober ❐ Intoxicated ❐ Has Been Drinking ❐ Drugs

Reported by
❐ Same ❐ N/A

Last name   First   Middle   Maiden

Address

Home phone   Email address

Gender   Date of Birth (Month/day/year)
❐ Male   ❐ Female

Marital status
❐ Single ❐ Married ❐ Common-law ❐ Widowed ❐ Divorced

Employer   Work phone

Work address

Condition ❐ Sober ❐ Intoxicated ❐ Has Been Drinking ❐ Drugs

Accused/Suspect

Last name   First   Middle   Maiden

(continued)

Figure 4.1 (continued)

Address

Home phone

Email address

Gender
☐ Male   ☐ Female

Date of Birth (Month/day/year)

Physical Description

Height

Weight

Hair Colour

Glasses ☐ Yes ☐ No

☐ Straight   ☐ Curly ☐ Wavy ☐ Bald
☐ Crew cut ☐ Pixie   ☐ Shoulder length ☐ Other

Facial Hair ☐ Clean-shaven ☐ Moustache ☐ Beard ☐ Goatee ☐ Other

Clothing

Distinguishing Features

Marital status
☐ Single ☐ Married ☐ Common-law ☐ Widowed ☐ Divorced

Employer

Work phone

Work address

(continued)

Driver's license number

[ ]

Relationship to victim/complainant

[ ]

Condition ☐ Sober ☐ Intoxicated ☐ Has Been Drinking ☐ Drugs

Charges

[ ]

Warrant Executed ☐ No ☐ Yes Type [ ]

CPIC Results ☐ Negative ☐ Priors

[ ]

Fingerprint Date   Form of release

[ ]   [ ]

Bail/Bond ☐ N/A [ ]

Date of release   Time of release

[ ]   [ ]   ☐ N/A

☐ Remand

Court Date

[ ]

Narrative/Summary

[ ]

Incident Status
☐ Open   ☐ Reassigned to [ ]
☐ Closed ☐ Solved ☐ Unsolved ☐ Unfounded

Reporting Officer

[ ]

Date of report   Time of report

[ ]   [ ]

Checked by [ ]

Incident Reports

An *incident report*, also referred to as a *General Occurrence Report* (GOR), is typically used to report any incident, other than a motor vehicle collision, that did not result in an immediate arrest. It is written in the past tense, since it is completed after an incident occurs. Present or future tense can be used to refer to current belief ("The suspect is considered armed and dangerous") or planned action (investigative activities that have not yet been carried out). An incident report is generally written in the third person ("Constable Green [as opposed to "I"] attended at 432 High Street"); the use of the third person conveys a sense of distance and impartiality that aids the report's credibility. Active voice is used. With active voice, the subject of a sentence is the actor ("I shot the sheriff"); with passive voice, the subject of the sentence is acted upon ("The sheriff was shot"). Passive voice can leave a sense of vagueness that is incompatible with clear, precise writing.

As mentioned, an incident report is written when an arrest has not occurred by the time the report is written. This report is completed by the first officer on the scene of an incident, and is submitted by the end of a shift. The GOR documents details of the incident and recounts police actions in relation to the occurrence up to that point. Since many incidents are not cleared immediately, an incident report is often supplemented by additional reports that cover the ongoing investigation. Any time there is a change, a new narrative, or supplemental, is written. These further reports might not be written by the original officer, since cases are often handed over to other patrol officers or to members of the Criminal Investigation Branch (detectives). Some cases are reassigned to special areas, such as the Sex Crimes Unit or Homicide. Supplemental reports are added until the case is cleared as solved, unsolved, or unfounded. Unsolved cases may be followed up by a cold case unit as new evidence arises.

There are two sections of an incident report: the cover page and narrative. The cover page contains a wealth of details that may aid the investigation and that can be used for analysis and data mining. Figure 4.2 provides a sample cover page for the incident whose narrative is provided on the next page. As mentioned above, the actual format of a cover page will vary by police service; the sample provides an example of common elements.

It might be thought that completing a cover page is easy, mindless work, especially if the document is electronic, with drop-down menu choices. However, completing it well so that it can be used by both investigators and crime analysis personnel is crucial to the organization's achieving its mission of not only solving crime but preventing crime through strategic intelligence-led policing. These cover pages are a major source of that intelligence.

The narrative of a GOR paints the picture and tells the story of an incident for the reader. Using complete sentences and conventional storytelling structure (context-setting, beginning, middle, and end), the writer recreates the occurrence:

> . . . When doing a report you have to imagine
> that you are painting a picture, so that when
> someone reads your report they understand what
> is happening.

Figure 4.2

GENERAL OCCURRENCE REPORT

Police Service Online Report Form

Report Type:

☑ General Occurrence Report
☐ Arrest Report
☐ Summons

Incident Number

02-26-2008-3341

Officer, Badge Number

MCHUGH, Darren
572

Date and Time of Incident

February 26, 2008
06:45

Incident Location

8 Alden Avenue

Weapon ☐ No ☐ Yes ☑ Unknown

Type

Unknown weapon/Tool used
to slash tires

Victim/Complainant

Last name	First	Middle	Maiden
EDWARDS	David		

Address

8 Alden Avenue
Toronto, Ontario
M8Z 1C5

Home phone

416-337-9923

Email address

davidedwards@gmail.com

Gender
☑ Male ☐ Female

Date of Birth (Month/day/year)

| 0 | 7 | 2 | 3 | 1 | 9 | 6 | 3 |

Marital status
☐ Single ☑ Married ☐ Common-law ☐ Widowed ☐ Divorced

Employer

Joe's Plumbing

Work phone

416-289-7333

(continued)

Work address

> 1067 Bloor Street West
> Toronto, Ontario
> M9X 3F3

Condition ☑ Sober ☐ Intoxicated ☐ Has Been Drinking ☐ Drugs

Reported by
☑ Same ☐ N/A

Last name   First   Middle   Maiden

Address

Home phone   Email address

Gender   Date of Birth (Month/day/year)
☐ Male   ☐ Female

Marital status
☐ Single ☐ Married ☐ Common-law ☐ Widowed ☐ Divorced

Employer   Work phone

Work address

Condition ☐ Sober ☐ Intoxicated ☐ Has Been Drinking ☐ Drugs

Accused/Suspect

Last name   First   Middle   Maiden

(continued)

Figure 4.2 (continued)

Address

Home phone   Email address

Gender   Date of Birth (Month/day/year)
☐ Male   ☐ Female

Physical Description
Height [   ]   Weight [   ]

Hair Colour [   ]   Glasses ☐ Yes ☐ No

☐ Straight   ☐ Curly   ☐ Wavy   ☐ Bald
☐ Crew cut   ☐ Pixie   ☐ Shoulder length   ☐ Other

Facial Hair ☐ Clean-shaven ☐ Moustache ☐ Beard ☐ Goatee ☐ Other

Clothing

Distinguishing Features

Marital status
☐ Single   ☐ Married   ☐ Common-law   ☐ Widowed   ☐ Divorced

Employer   Work phone

Work address

(continued)

Driver's license number

Relationship to victim/complainant

Condition ☐ Sober ☐ Intoxicated ☐ Has Been Drinking ☐ Drugs

Charges

Warrant Executed ☐ No ☐ Yes Type

CPIC Results ☐ Negative ☐ Priors

Fingerprint Date   Form of release

Bail/Bond ☐ N/A

Date of release   Time of release
                                              ☐ N/A

☐ Remand

Court Date

Narrative/Summary

see below: Incident report narrative

Incident Status
☑ Open   ☐ Reassigned to
☐ Closed ☐ Solved ☑ Unsolved ☐ Unfounded

Reporting Officer
MCHUGH, Darren 572

Date of report   Time of report
February 26, 2008   13:20

Checked by | MATTHEWS, Sheila 356

Below is an example of the narrative section of an incident report, written by a student in Humber College's Police Foundations program.

Incident Report Narrative

At 06:34 hours on Tuesday February 26, 2008 Constable McHugh responded to a dispatched call at 8 Alden Avenue Toronto. The call regarded David Edwards who said the tires of his car had been slashed.

Upon arrival at 06:45 hours the writer was met by David Edwards outside the front of his home and reported the following. David Edwards is 45 years old and is married to Joanne Edwards who is 41 years old. They have 2 children, John and Stephen, who are 10 and 6 years old. Mr. Edwards is a manager and works at Joe's Plumbing located at 1067 Bloor Street West, Toronto. Mrs. Edwards is a doctor and works at Toronto General Hospital located at 385 University Avenue, Toronto. Mr. and Mrs. Edwards own the house at 8 Alden Avenue that is a detached bungalow with 4 bedrooms and a double car garage. Alden Avenue is a small street with 14 houses on each side of the street located in a suburban area.

Mr. Edwards walked out of his house at 06:30 hours on his way to work. When he got to his driveway where his car was parked on the left side, he noticed that all 4 tires were flat. He stated that the last time he saw his car was the previous day at 18:30 hours when he returned home from work.

Mr. Edwards's car is a silver 4 door Honda Accord with dark tinted windows, licence plate # AGDR 157, VIN # 358305782. All 4 tires had a 1 inch slice on the wall of the tire. Mrs. Edwards's car, parked on the right side of the driveway, was not damaged.

Constable McHugh canvassed Alden Avenue but found no witnesses or damage to any other vehicles. Mr. Edwards reported a possible suspect. He described the events of yesterday, Monday, February 25, 2008, at 07:30 hours at Joe's Plumbing when an employee named Billy Johnson arrived at work with alcohol on his breath and appeared to be intoxicated. Mr. Edwards explained that Mr. Johnson had been warned in the past about his behaviour and fired him. After Edwards asked him to leave the property, Mr. Johnson called Mr. Edwards an asshole and kicked over a chair before exiting the building.

Billy Johnson's home address is apt.606, 1526 River Drive, Toronto, former shipping receiving employee at Joe's Plumbing.

At 11:50 hours Tuesday February 26, 2008 Constable McHugh attempted to contact Mr. Johnson at his home with negative results.

Investigation continues.

Constable Darren McHugh #572
February 26, 2008 13:20 hours

Source: Courtesy of Darren McHugh.

Table 4.1 contains a criteria sheet for incident report evaluation. Again, your teacher may choose to use or modify this criteria sheet.

Table 4.1

INCIDENT REPORT EVALUATION

	Fail	Minimum Pass	Solid Pass	Pass with Excellence
Written in third person				
Written in past tense				
Written in active voice				
Uses precise details				
Written in complete sentences				
Correct grammar and spelling				
Follows narrative sequence				
Overall quality and usefulness of narrative				

Arrest Reports

Arrest reports detail the arrest of a suspect. An arrest may occur when a crime has been committed. There are several elements to the definition of a crime.

What Is a Crime?

A *crime* is generally defined as an act or omission that is prohibited by criminal law.... Two critical ingredients of a crime are the commission of an act (*actus reus*) and the mental intent to commit the act (*mens rea*). A crime occurs when a person:

- commits an act or fails to commit an act when under a legal responsibility to do so;

- has the intent, or *mens rea,* to commit the act;

- does not have a legal defence or justification for committing the act; *and*

- violates a provision in criminal law.

Source: From Griffiths, K. (2006). *Canadian Criminal Justice: A Primer,* pp. 24–25. Toronto: Nelson.

An officer is concerned with the facts-in-issue of an offence, those things that indicate that a crime has indeed occurred.

Figure 4.3 offers the several possible paths that might be taken to compel an accused person to trial.

An arrest can occur immediately if an offender is *found committing* the criminal action by a police officer; if a suspect is not found committing, reasonable cause must be shown for an arrest warrant to be issued by a justice of the peace. (The same is true for a search to occur; a warrantless search except during an arrest can usually be successfully appealed).

Figure 4.3

CRIMINAL INCIDENTS

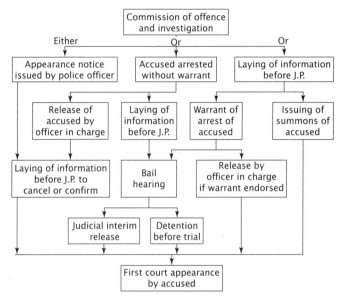

Source: From Mewett, A.W., and S. Nakatsuru. (2001). *An Introduction to the Criminal Process in Canada,* 4th ed., p. 72. Toronto: Carswell. Reprinted by permission of Carswell, a division of Thomson Reuters Canada Limited.

An arrest report, similar to the GOR, consists of two parts: a cover page and narrative. The cover page is similar to that of an incident report, with the addition of details regarding the charge and disposition.

The narrative of an arrest report depends on whether the suspect has been found committing, or if the arrest is after the fact. If the offence is in progress when the officer arrives, and the suspect is successfully apprehended, the arrest report takes the place of the incident report. The arrest report recreates the occurrence and provides justification for the arrest, as well as documenting the arrest process, to show that the suspect's rights were not violated. If the arrest is after the fact, as a result of a warrant, the arrest report refers back to the original GOR and any supplemental reports, and documents the arrest. The type of warrant is always mentioned because the legitimacy of a belated arrest depends on the appropriate execution of a particular warrant. For example, to enter a dwelling house to arrest a suspect, an officer needs a Feeney warrant, named after "R. vs. Feeney," the case referred to in Chapter 2.

The most common use of an arrest report is when a guilty plea is entered. The narrative portion of the arrest report is entered into the record. Along with witness statements, the narrative portion of an arrest report is included in the Crown Brief.

Figure 4.4 is an example of the cover page and narrative of an arrest report, based on the continuing saga of the above incident. The witness statement example below will also refer to this scenario. (Again, the example given is based on common elements of arrest reports; actual reports vary by police service.)

Figure 4.4

ARREST REPORT

Police Service Online Report Form

Report Type:

☐ General Occurrence Report
☑ Arrest Report
☐ Summons

Incident Number

02-26-2008-3385

Officer, Badge Number

HAMWADI, Ali
2431

Date and Time of Incident

Feb. 26, 2008
19:30

Incident Location

8 Alden Avenue

Weapon ☐ No ☑ Yes ☐ Unknown

Type

Wooden baseball bat

Victim/Complainant

Last name	First	Middle	Maiden
EDWARDS	David		

Address

8 Alden Avenue
Toronto, Ontario
M8Z 1C5

Home phone	Email address
416-337-9923	davidedwards@gmail.com

Gender
☑ Male   ☐ Female

Date of Birth (Month/day/year)

| 0 | 7 | 2 | 3 | 1 | 9 | 6 | 3 |

Marital status
☐ Single ☑ Married ☐ Common-law ☐ Widowed ☐ Divorced

Employer	Work phone
Joe's Plumbing	416-289-7333

(continued)

Figure 4.4 (continued)

Work address

1067 Bloor St. W.
Toronto, Ontario
M9X 3F3

Condition ☑ Sober ☐ Intoxicated ☐ Has Been Drinking ☐ Drugs

Reported by
☐ Same   ☐ N/A

Last name	First	Middle	Maiden

HARRISON   Melissa

Address

10 Alden Avenue
Toronto, Ontario
M8Z 1C5

Home phone	Email address

416-259-5531   melissaharrison07@hotmail.com

Gender   Date of Birth (Month/day/year)
☐ Male   ☑ Female | 0 | 4 | 0 | 4 | 1 | 9 | 8 | 8 |

Marital status
☑ Single ☐ Married ☐ Common-law ☐ Widowed ☐ Divorced

Employer	Work phone

Precious Gems Jewellery   905-828-8822

Work address

271 Tourmaline Way
Mississauga, Ontario
L5D 2B6

Condition ☑ Sober ☐ Intoxicated ☐ Has Been Drinking ☐ Drugs

Accused/Suspect

Last name	First	Middle	Maiden

JOHNSON   Billy

(continued)

Address

1526 River Drive, Apt. 806
Toronto, Ontario
M7D 3V5

Home phone

416-921-2374

Email address

haveabrew27@yahoo.ca

Gender
☑ Male   ❑ Female

Date of Birth (Month/day/year)

| 0 | 9 | 1 | 5 | 1 | 9 | 8 | 2 |

Physical Description

Height | 5 ft. 10 in. | Weight | 170 lb. |

Hair Colour | brown | Glasses ❑ Yes ☑ No

☑ Straight   ❑ Curly   ❑ Wavy   ❑ Bald
❑ Crew cut   ❑ Pixie   ☑ Shoulder length   ❑ Other

Facial Hair ❑ Clean-shaven ❑ Moustache ❑ Beard ❑ Goatee ☑ Other

unshaven (5 o'clock shadow)

Clothing

black denim jeans, black cotton tee shirt, black Nike
runners, black leather jacket

Distinguishing Features

1 inch horizontal scar over right eyebrow

Marital status
☑ Single   ❑ Married   ❑ Common-law   ❑ Widowed   ❑ Divorced

Employer

unemployed

Work phone

Work address

(continued)

Figure 4.4 (continued)

Driver's license number

revoked

Relationship to victim/complainant

former employee

Condition ☐ Sober ☐ Intoxicated ☐ Has Been Drinking ☐ Drugs

Charges

267 Assault with weapon causing bodily harm; 430.1 Mischief

Warrant Executed ☑ No ☐ Yes Type

CPIC Results ☐ Negative ☐ Priors

3 DUI convictions in past two years
License revoked 02/09/2007

Fingerprint Date   Form of release

Bail/Bond ☐ N/A

Date of release   Time of release

☐ N/A

☑ Remand

Court Date

Narrative/Summary

On February 26, 2008 at 19:25 Cst. Ali HEMWADI responded to
8 Alden Avenue regarding a 911 call. Upon arrival at 19:30 the
officer was met by Melissa HARRISON, resident at 10 Alden
Avenue. HARRISON had placed the 911 call after hearing
breaking glass, loud noises, and seeing a man about 5 ft. 10
inches tall, weighing about 165 pounds, and wearing black
denim jeans and a black leather jacket enter the side door of 8
Alden Avenue carrying a wooden baseball bat. As she waited for
police arrival, she heard shouting from the inside of 8 Alden
Avenue. Cst. HEMWADI observed a silver 4 door Honda Accord,
license plate AGDR 157, parked in the driveway of the house.
The car had 4 new tires. Front passenger door was dented and
front windshield was shattered.
Shouting could be heard inside 8 Alden Avenue. This writer
knocked loudly on the side door, which was ajar. There was no
answer. Writer heard a woman scream and announced he was
entering the dwelling. Three people were in the front room of
the house. The writer observed Joanne EDWARDS kneeling beside

(continued)

her husband, screaming and weeping as the suspect, Billy JOHNSON, hit a 4 inch plasma television with a wooden baseball bat. David EDWARDS lay on his back on the floor perpendicular to the television set. There was a three-inch gash on his forehead consistent with a blow from a heavy object.

This writer directed JOHNSON to drop the baseball bat and turn around. JOHNSON dropped the bat, raised his hands to the air, turned around and extended his hands in front of his chest, inside of wrists together. Writer placed restraints on his wrist and stated that he was under arrest for assault with a weapon causing bodily harm and mischief. Writer checked David EDWARDS for vital signs and called for an ambulance along with crime scene backup and prisoner transport. EDWARDS opened his eyes but did not respond when asked if he was alright.

This writer then read JOHNSON the caution and right to counsel from the writer's memo book and asked if he understood. JOHNSON smiled and said, "Hell, yeah. The bastard deserved it. Who needs his f----ing job?" JOHNSON had been fired by EDWARDS for coming to work intoxicated. See 02-26-2008-3341 for GOR.

Joanne EDWARDS recounted that after dropping her two children at a Scouts meeting at 19:00, she and her husband had been watching television. At approximately 19:15 they heard banging and breaking glass outside in their driveway. David EDWARDS got up from his chair to investigate as JOHNSON entered the house through the unlocked side door, carrying a baseball bat. JOHNSON hit the husband in the forehead with the bat, causing him to fall to the floor. JOHNSON began to hit furniture with the bat. This writer observed two shattered table lamps, a two inch gouge in the top of a wooden coffee table and a dent in the upper right border of the television set.

Ambulance arrived at 19:45 and paramedics transported EDWARDS, accompanied by wife. Prisoner transport arrived at 19:50. JOHNSON was taken to 22 Division for questioning and lock-up. This writer interviewed witness Melissa HARRISON, and returned to 22 Division at 20:30.

Incident Status
❑ Open   ❑ Reassigned to [   ]
☑ Closed ☑ Solved ❑ Unsolved ❑ Unfounded

Reporting Officer

HEMWADI, Ali

Date of report	Time of report
Feb. 26, 2008	21:00

Checked by | WILLIAMS, Ermina

Table 4.2 contains a criteria sheet for the arrest report.

Table 4.2

ARREST REPORT EVALUATION

	Fail	Minimum Pass	Solid Pass	Pass with Excellence
Cover page				
Setting up of narrative				
Appropriate structure for type of arrest (in process or as result of warrant)				
Includes details for lawful arrest (caution, right to counsel, etc.)				
Quality and usefulness of narrative				
Correct grammar and spelling				
Precise language				

Witness Statements

Formal witness statements have several uses. At the time of the investigation, they provide details that can be added to other known information to help officers solve a case. As Toronto Police Chief Bill Blair told an audience at the community meeting mentioned in Chapter 2, an investigation is like a puzzle. Individual witnesses have some pieces to add to the puzzle. Each piece may not seem important to the witness, and therefore not worth sharing with police, but when combined with the rest of the puzzle pieces, a clear picture could emerge for investigators.

Witness statements are also used to establish reasonable grounds for search and/or arrest warrants. In addition, if a case goes to trial, a witness can refresh his or her memory of the incident before testifying by rereading the witness statement. In rare cases, a judge can allow the witness statement to be admitted into evidence. For example, when a witness is unavailable due to illness, death, or serious legitimate conflict, the witness statement might be allowed as a substitute for that testimony in order to keep the administration of justice from being brought into disrepute.

Witnesses dictate their statement to an officer, who cannot lead the witness but can ask probing questions to bring out relevant details. After dictating the statement, the witness reads it over, corrects any inaccuracies by crossing out the error with one line and initialling the correction, and signs the statement. The officer signs the statement as well, and records the time and location the statement was taken, along with who was present. Witnesses are always interviewed separately to avoid contamination of evidence. As with all police documents, no blank lines are left in a witness statement. The statement is written on every line.

Since the witness statement is a recounting of what a particular witness could testify to under oath, witness statements typically begin with a conventional heading: "[Witness name] will say." They are written in the first person, and begin by giving personal information about the witness to help establish credibility.

Below is an example of a witness statement.

Witness Statement

Melissa Harrison will say:

I am Melissa Harrison. I am 20 years old. I have lived at 10 Alden Avenue with my parents for 18 years. I work full-time at Precious Gems Jewellery as a clerk and attend Sheridan College part-time in the Developmental Services Worker program. I have lived beside and known David and Joanne Edwards for 15 years.

On February 26, 2008 I returned from work at 6:00 p.m. My parents were both out of town on vacation. After preparing and eating dinner I sat at the dining room table at about 6:45 to study for a test. The dining room has a bay window that looks out on the Edwards driveway and side door. After about twenty minutes to a half hour I heard breaking glass and loud noises and saw a man about 5 feet 10 inches tall and weighing about 160 or 170 pounds. The man was wearing black jeans and a black leather jacket and carrying a wooden baseball bat. It was the thicker kind that you play softball with. I could see that the front windshield of the Edwards car was broken. The man went to the Edwards side door and pushed it open. I immediately called 911 on my cell phone.

I was afraid to go over to the Edwards house by myself to help, so I waited on my front porch until a police cruiser arrived. I told the officer what I had seen. He called into the Edwards house and then went into the house through the side door, which the man had left partly open. About five minutes later an ambulance arrived, as well as another police car. The ambulance took David away; Joanne went along with him in the ambulance after I told her that I would pick up their two children from Scouts at 8:30 and put them to bed at my house. I then gave the officer this statement about the incident.

Melissa Harrison
Ali Hemwadi
Time interview began: 20:00
Time interview ended: 20:15
Location: 10 Alden Avenue
Present: Melissa Harrison, Ali Hemwadi

A criteria sheet for the witness statement can be found in Table 4.3, followed by Explorations for this chapter.

Table 4.3

WITNESS STATEMENT EVALUATION

	Fail	Minimum Pass	Solid Pass	Pass with Excellence
Conventional heading				
Precise details				
Narrative structure: Context				
Narrative structure: Events leading up to incident				
Narrative structure: Events during incident				
Narrative structure: Events after incident				
Required signatures (witness, officer) and notations: • time began • time ended • location • persons present				

EXPLORATIONS

4.1 In the United States, Florida state law requires law enforcement agencies, in the interest of public safety and general crime deterrence, to publish information about all arrests made. Several jurisdictions publish that information on the Internet. Go to the following website at http://sarasotasheriff.org/arrests.asp. The website lists all persons arrested in Sarasota County, Florida, on a given day. Select one person listed on that website. Using the Arrest Report form (same as GOR), write an arrest report for the offender. You will need to create additional details beyond the website information. Hand in a printout of the website page for your offender to your teacher with your arrest report.

4.2 You are called to a domestic disturbance. When you arrive, you find a man and his wife on the sidewalk in front of their home. The husband is screaming at his wife while slapping her. The wife bears physical signs of assault. Write the following three witness statements:

    a. A statement from the couple's next-door neighbour, an elderly woman who saw the husband when he came home. She can testify to his behaviour before the offence, as well as offer some details of the offence itself.

    b. A statement from the person who called in the disturbance. That person had been walking her dog when she observed the assault.

    c. Your own witness statement, since the offence was in progress when you arrived at the scene.

4.3 Write a either a general occurrence *or* an arrest report for the incident in Exploration 2.

4.4 Use an incident from the newspaper or television news as a source for a GOR.

4.5 Use an incident from the newspaper or television news as a source for a witness statement.

4.6 Use an incident from the newspaper or television news as a source for an arrest report.

4.7 Use an incident from your notebook assignment in Chapter 3 (page 67) as a source for a GOR or arrest report. Do not invent any additional details beyond what you have recorded in your notebook.

4.8 Write an arrest report based on "Mary's Arrest" on the course website.

Chapter 5

Internal Police Communication: Memorandums

In any organization, memos or e-mails are used to communicate internally. Letters or e-mails are used for external communication. Police services generally have a template for memorandum communication. The template would include the following standard parts of a memo:

```
To:
From:
Subject:
Date:
```

These headings are used in any organization, although in some organizations "Subject" might be replaced by "Re" [regarding].

The memo text itself is single-spaced, with no paragraph indents. Paragraphs tend to be short, and a line is left blank between paragraphs. Outside policing organizations, memos are not signed, because the "to" line indicates who the author of the memo is. However, in some policing organizations, memos are always signed, and the writer's rank is also given. This may have something to do with the chain-of-command culture that can often be found in a police service. When on the job, you would follow the practice within your organization.

In non-policing organizations, a memo writer will decide on one of two approaches, depending on the audience's probable response to the memo's message. A *direct* approach will be used when the audience is expected to be positively inclined or neutral to the memo's content; an *indirect* approach is used if the audience is expected to be opposed to the memo's message (sometimes referred to as "bad news"). In police services, however, most memos take a direct approach regardless of the readers' anticipated response. This too can be attributed to the police "command and control" culture. While some organizations are changing, the predominant sentiment within the police service may still be that it doesn't matter whether members like or dislike what the writer is about to say—they have to do what their superior says anyway, so the writer gets straight to the point.

Almost all the memos in this chapter were written by practising police officers (the exception is the memo on the "24-7 Lecture on Domestic Violence"). For each, consider the memo's context, the situation the memo addresses, the language used, and the approach chosen.

The first memo below highlights a problem the writer has noticed. The writer makes what he calls a somewhat unusual request, but backs up the request logically and persuasively.

Re: Non-Budgeted Items for One-Time Purchase

Internal Correspondence

TO: S/Supt. G. Grant   FROM: S/Sgt. Scott Roberts
    Officer in Charge   #359
    Operational   Public Safety Unit
    Support   DATE: June 28, 2007

We are requesting the purchase of replacement water coolers for installation at the Public Safety Unit.

Over the past two years we have noted a decrease in the performance of personnel assigned to the Public Safety Unit. This decrease appears to have commenced and gradually worsened after the removal of the water coolers that had been deemed inoperable. At the time of their removal it was determined that funds were not available to replace the devices.

Direct approach: Request made immediately

Reason

Emphasis

This request may seem unconventional, but it is being made with a strong sense of urgency.

Benefits
and details

The ability of our personnel to informally meet and discuss problematic issues has been replaced with structured meetings and set agendas that seldom result in completed tasks. Incomplete work has proven to be a divisive factor for our team, and is the primary cause of our diminished performance and morale. The purchase and installation of two water coolers will create an inviting, informal atmosphere where the spirits of our staff will flourish. The quoted cost of $579.00, as attached, is a small investment with a substantial return for the Unit and the Service.

Contact
info

If you would like further details please contact me at 8-4921

Scott Roberts
S/Sgt #359
PSU-EM

Source: Courtesy of Staff Sergeant Scott Roberts.

Notice the structure of this first memo. The writer begins immediately with the actual request (direct approach). He then goes into the background of the request, in this case, the problem that will be resolved by approving the request. He then gives the benefits of making this change, which is actually just going back to an earlier practice. He also gives details about the request, in this case, the cost. He ends with contact information.

This structure is fairly standard for request or problem–solution memos. See if you can see this underlying structure in the following longer, more complex memo. This next memo (below) details a proposed solution to a problem in one of Canada's major cities, along with a strategy to defuse the resistance that his solution, a zero-tolerance parking policy, would cause. The writer does not downplay the negative reaction such a change would generate, but is clear about the benefits of accepting his suggestion; most importantly, he is able to proactively present a strategy that could forestall any objections by the public to the stepped-up parking enforcement.

Internal Correspondence

TO: SUPERINTENDENT   FROM: Bill BOSWARD
    UNIT COMMANDER   STAFF SERGEANT #6190
                        DATE: 2007/06/25

RE: COMMUNICATING NEW CORPORATE POLICY, PARKING
    STRATEGIES

Within the City of Toronto, traffic volume and congestion have become major problems for residents. It is estimated that over 250,000 vehicles per day enter Toronto. Major arterial roadways have reached maximum capacity with traffic flow.

Indirect approach: complex issue, underlying problem

Associated with traffic volume and congestion is parking for commuters. Several options are available. Public parking lots are present within the boundaries of Toronto for commuters to park in. Police are called to these locations by the custodians to enforce parking infractions.

Associated problems and options

Also available are off-street private parking facilities. These facilities are privately funded, policed, and parking infractions enforced by hired private security guards.

A third option available to the commuter is on-street pay and display parking. As you know, this is where the commuter parks in a designated on-street parking spot, purchases a parking receipt from a machine, and displays the receipt on the dashboard of their vehicle. This area of parking is enforced by local Parking Enforcement Officers.

It is the latter, on-street pay and display parking, that is causing partial traffic congestion within the downtown core of the City.

Problem with third option

It is proposed that to alleviate some of the traffic congestion experienced within Toronto, a new corporate policy of zero tolerance for all vehicle parking infractions be issued. This would include

Suggestion and details

strict enforcement of all pay and display parking, high enforcement of all bylaw infractions, such as parking in other than designated parking locations, removing the 10-minute grace period for all courier and delivery vehicles blocking the free flow of traffic, and heavy enforcement of all on-street overtime 3-hour parking.

Strategy to deal with negative reaction

To combat the intense media scrutiny expected from this new policy, it is proposed that a corporate communications strategy be developed and communicated to the media explaining the need for the free flow of commuter traffic. Part of this communications strategy should be to inform the public of the imposed health risks associated with idling vehicles, as well as the fact that documented road rage incidents are on the increase. It is believed this is a result of increased stress while waiting in traffic.

Benefits

Corporate business partnerships should also be sought to support this policy. Their perspective would be centred on lost production and lost revenue that could be avoided if commuters were able to travel to work without obstructions.

The new policy should be tracked for a trial period of one year and then be evaluated for its effectiveness.

In conclusion, it is felt that if the above strategies were implemented, the residents of Toronto, the commuters to Toronto, and the corporate business community would all benefit from our policy change. The resulting side effect of increased revenue in the form of additional parking tickets issued would also be noticed by the City of Toronto.

With Regards,
Bill Bosward
Staff Sergeant #6190

Source: Courtesy of Bill Bosward, Staff Sergeant #6190.

Another common type of memo is a policy memo: announcing, clarifying, or reiterating a policy in the organization. Here are three memos that deal with the same issue (the need to control overtime expenditures) and resulting policy in somewhat different ways. Each is effectively written for a specific audience and illustrates that there are many effective approaches to writing about a situation. Consider the differences in these memos.

Internal Correspondence

TO: Section Heads   FROM: Tony Riviere
     53 Division   S/Sgt 918 53 Division
                     DATE: 2007/06/21

RE: Communicating Need to Control Staff Overtime

According to the Dashboard Report for the month of June, our Division has utilized 90 percent of its allocated annual overtime budget. As a result, I am implementing a series of actions intended to monitor and control the allotment of overtime.

> Direct approach: Problem and resulting policy

Over the past three months we have been confronted with a number of unforeseen incidents that have seriously impacted our resources. Investigations resulting from a homicide at 24 Elm Street in the month of February, the home invasion at 33 Merkley Avenue in May, and the gas explosion at 1250 Yonge Street have resulted in a significant accumulation of overtime. This series of incidents has resulted in the utilization of 90 percent of our annual overtime budget and we are only at the mid-point of the year.

> Reasons for problem

In order to efficiently manage the remainder of our overtime budget, I am instructing that the following be instituted immediately:

> Details of policy

- Major Crime unit will be restricted to perform their duties solely on a Dayshift, unless prior approval is received from the unit commander.

- Platoon commanders shall ensure that all approved overtime assignments are captured on the unit-specific overtime form and include a detailed explanation of reasons for overtime and options considered.

- All non-primary response units shall perform short-term strategic planning to ensure officers' shift schedules are modified to accommodate events that may result in overtime expenditure. Strategies are to be forwarded to the unit commander for prior approval.

- Primary response units working the Night shift shall supply two officers to complement the busier Evening shift.

- Until further notice, Lieu time will only be granted upon the approval of the unit commander.

Sensitive close

I appreciate that these measures are drastic and may cause temporary hardship to some personnel. However, it is essential that these steps be implemented in order for us to maintain an acceptable level of efficient service to the community.

Thanks in advance for your contributions.

Tony Riviere
Staff Sergeant 918
53 Community Response Unit

Source: Courtesy of Tony Riviere.

Memorandum

To:	Platoon Staff Sergeants 43 Division	From:	Superintendent B.I.G. Hammer 43 Division
		Date:	2007/06/24

Re: Controlling Overtime

Problem

It has become apparent that overtime pay projections for the division in the current fiscal year have greatly exceeded our stated budgetary goals.

Reason for problem

The excesses are a result of a number of unprecedented incidents such as the ongoing violent labour strike at the ACME Nut Bar factory and an unusually high number of gang-related shootings and homicides.

It is understood that unexpected operational necessities such as the strike and gang activity put a significant strain on our personal and resources. Nevertheless, it is incumbent upon all platoon commanders to make every effort in their daily managing of platoon activities to monitor overtime approvals to minimize unnecessary costs. Platoon commanders are directed to review and approve, in writing, overtime on a case-by-case basis.

Policy

As members of the management team, platoon commanders will be held accountable for approved overtime through a daily overtime report. This report will indicate the involved officers, number of hours incurred, the incident number, and a brief explanation as to why the overtime was necessary. This report will be signed by the platoon Staff Sergeant approving the overtime and will be made available to the unit commander at 0700 hrs every day for inclusion in the morning report and morning meeting.

Details

Any questions should be referred to Inspector B.E. Apain at Loc 8-4300.

Contact info

B.I.G. Hammer
Superintendent
43 Division
BH/al

Source: Courtesy of D/Sgt. Art Little, #935 Professional Standards.

Internal Correspondence

TO: Staff Superintendent T. Corrie
       Professional Standards
FROM: Deputy S. Richardson # 5513
       Executive Command
DATE: 2007/06/22

RE: New Procedure for Approval of Overtime

Effective immediately, members of Professional Standards (PRS) will be required to adhere to a new overtime approval process. This has been developed

Policy and reason

as a result of a recent audit and review of your premium pay accounts. The audit conducted June 21, 2007, determined that your overtime budget is projected to exceed the designated funding for this account.

The following five (5) step procedure shall be followed at all times when overtime is anticipated to occur:

1. Prior to the completion of his/her shift, sworn members will notify a PRS Supervisor in the event that an emergent, unplanned circumstance has occurred and overtime may be required to resolve the incident or investigation.
2. The PRS Supervisor will review the circumstance, determine if there are any alternative methods to resolve the incident, and decide if overtime is necessary.
3. If overtime is to be authorized, the supervisor will record the details in his memorandum book and complete an Overtime Authorization Form (TPS 555).
4. The Supervisor shall note any corresponding ICAD event number, complainant name, or witness name within the comments section of the TPS 555.
5. The TPS 555 form will be signed by the authorizing supervisor and forwarded to the Unit Commander for review.

In the event Supervisors and sworn members do not adhere to this policy, overtime incurred will not be authorized or paid.

Please distribute this memorandum forthwith to members in your unit. If you have any questions or concerns regarding this memorandum, please do not hesitate to contact me at (416) 808-7725.

Sandra Richardson
Deputy Chief
Toronto Police Service

Source: Courtesy of Sandra Richardson.

Despite their differences, the above policy memos share a common structure. They begin with background relevant to the policy addressed. They give the context for the policy, highlighting the issue the policy deals with. They go on to give details of the policy, although in different ways and depths based on their audience's needs and the situation. They then close. Notice the differences in the closings. How does each closing fit the situation and the audience addressed?

The next memo is also a policy memo, and deals with a delicate problem. The writer is the Unit Commander of a mounted and police dog unit. Horses are a valuable asset to a police department, but they do have one drawback—horses poo. And sometimes a member of the public complains. This is an internal memo dealing with the policy that tries to forestall those complaints; for a letter responding to such a complaint, see the following chapter. Both deal in a clear, professional way with this issue. This memo shares the typical policy memo structure: background, policy details, close.

Internal Correspondence

TO: All Personnel   FROM: Staff Inspector
     Mounted Unit   Bill Wardle
                             Unit Commander—
                             Mounted and PDS
                      DATE: 2007/06/20

RE: Horse Manure

Complaints regarding horse manure have increased over the past months. The extension of patrols in 52 Division takes our horses into new communities who are unfamiliar with the sight of mounted officers on their streets. This issue is important for both the police and community. It is imperative that officers work to resolve and prevent these complaints from occurring.

Background to policy reminder: Why now?

Policy
details

Officers are reminded they should avoid riding on the sidewalk, footpaths, or bicycle paths unless necessary in the performance of their duty. If a horse does defecate in these areas, or in any other area where the public may be adversely affected, the officer should make every attempt to have the manure removed. The officer may dismount and personally remove it if safe conditions exist. If not, the duty supervisor at Mounted Headquarters may request a City works crew.

Reasons

Complaints regarding manure received by Mounted Headquarters are to be directed to the on-duty supervisor. The supervisor is responsible for conducting an immediate investigation. If the manure is on the sidewalk, footpath, bicycle path, private property, or in their opinion adversely affects the public, they are to arrange to have it removed. The supervisor will contact the City works department emergency number to have a crew dispatched to the scene. If a crew is unavailable, the stable manager can be utilized for the cleanup.

Every member of the Unit is responsible for ensuring that we maintain the trust and support of the community. The number of complaints received indicates that this is a significant issue for citizens. It is important that the community understand our position on the issue and that we do respond in an appropriate manner. By far, the most important factor in resolving such complaints is the attitude of the officer involved, whether at the scene or later by telephone.

The issue of horse manure has generated negative media coverage, public opinion, and political opinion in the past. If we are not sensitive to the complaints and the concerns of the community, we may find restrictions placed on us. Officers must be professional at all times and work with the community to ensure that this issue is addressed to everyone's satisfaction.

Source: Courtesy of William Wardle.

Announcements are another common memo type. The following memo announces an upcoming event, and proposes two different ways of participating in the event. Its primary purpose is to invite supervisors to attend the event in person, but it also serves as a reminder to encourage those reporting to them to watch it after the fact on tape. Because this is a well-known semi-annual event, the author uses a direct approach. (Note: This memo utilizes an alternative heading format to many in this chapter to illustrate that, so long as all four pieces of information are given, memo headings can differ.)

```
TO:       Supervisory personnel
FROM:     Sheila Songaard, Training Department
SUBJECT:  24-7 Lecture on Domestic Violence
DATE:     April 2, 2008
```

Invitation

I would like to invite you to attend the next 24-7 Lecture being held on June 10th, 2008 at 1300 hours.

Background

As you may know, the 24-7 Lecture is an innovative lecture series that is held twice a year in the auditorium of Police Headquarters located at 40 College Street. The lecture involves the participation of twenty-four different speakers, who are given seven minutes each to present their topic. The fast paced concept has been proven to provide a wide variety of important topics in a short period of time.

Details

The theme for this 24-7 Lecture will be Saving Our Youth. The speakers will include experts from the medical field, legal field, social services and police officers, as well as former teen gang members and an expert on in-school shootings.

The lecture will be taped and distributed to all officers through a video link on our internal computer system. Officers will be able to view the lecture at any time during their shift, so please encourage your units to do so.

RSVP and contact info

Please consider attending this upcoming lecture in person. To reserve a spot, RSVP by return email by August 14, 2008. If you have questions or wish further details, I can be reached at 7-8865.

The next memo is written to provide information about an event to a superior officer. This memo informs the unit commander of a past series of events. The unit commander needs to be told about a problem that had been discovered, the steps taken to alleviate the problem, and the results. While not strictly speaking an announcement, the memo follows the structure of supplying background, needed details, and a close.

Internal Correspondence

TO: INSPECTOR ANDRETTI   FROM: SHAUN WHITE
    #3447   #99854
    UNIT COMMANDER   SUPERVISOR—SUPERIOR
    COURT SERVICES   COURT
                          DATE: 2007/06/20

RE: HEALTH AND WELLNESS INITIATIVE

Sir,

Problem

Over the past few months, Superior Court has been faced with the increased and undue hardship in staffing due to an increase in the number of members off on sick time.

Initial review

After reviewing the sick reports over the last few months, all members that have been sick more than three (3) times were counselled, and offered the assistance of M.A.S., E.F.A.P., and general guidance as required.

Underlying issue

It was during these counselling sessions that the lack of insight and knowledge on general health and wellness on the part of staff became a resounding area of concern.

Steps taken

As a result, the TPS Health and Wellness co-ordinator, Kim Smith, and the Service-contracted registered Nutritionist, Lisa Jones, were contacted. Both Kim Smith and Lisa Jones were more than happy to attend Superior Court on two different dates to address all our Officers and provide this most needed information.

On Tuesday, June 19th, 2007, Lisa Jones attended Superior Court and presented the Officers with a very interactive and informative presentation on nutrition and the importance of healthy eating. She provided a lengthy question and answer period, along with informative handouts and material.

On Wednesday, June 20th, 2007, Kim Smith attended Superior Court and presented the Officers with an excellent health and wellness lecture that went over all areas of health including exercise, nutrition, vitamin supplementation, sleep, and positive attitude.

Each of these presentations was very well received by all of our members. Officers have commented to me and to the Supervisory Staff that it was the most informative and relevant information they had received to date. Since the presentations, the number of sick occurrences has decreased, and the morale has noticeably improved.

Results

It is my hope that this training and information continues to assist Superior Court in the areas of health, morale, and sick absenteeism.

Regards,

Shaun White
Supervisor #99854
Superior Court
(416) 224-5565

The following memo announces an organizational review. As you can see from the writer's discussion of the process, the review will involve a fair amount of work and might conceivably result in resistance, both for that reason and because of the perennial human tendency to be wary of change. Notice how the writer forestalls opposition through a positive tone, the sharing of the reasons this particular division was chosen to participate in the review, and a discussion of how the results of the review will be used. The close is especially interesting, as he does not directly order the officers to cooperate in the review; instead, he states his expectation of cooperation indirectly, although still clearly.

Internal Correspondence

TO: Members   FROM: Staff Superintendent
    X Division   M. Federico
                         X Division
                DATE: 2007/06/18

RE: Divisional Review

Announce-ment

I am pleased to announce that our division has been selected to participate in an organizational review. The review will help determine the optimal divisional structure necessary for the Service to deliver policing to the community. It will examine, among other things, management processes, frontline service delivery, investigative and support operations, staffing and deployment, as well as records and information systems, in an effort to determine best practices.

Why division selected

Our division was selected because, due to its size and complexity, it is considered representative of the Service in general. In the same way, the community we police is considered representative of most neighbourhoods in Toronto. Consequently, we believe the findings from this review will be relevant and applicable to the Service more generally.

Process

A team has been assembled to conduct the review using such methodologies as inspections, surveys, interviews, and scholarly research. On September 11, 2007, the review team will start its field work, under the direction of Staff Inspector Senior Officer. The team will conduct extensive individual interviews with our divisional personnel and other Service members. Data collection is expected to extend into the early part of next year. Focus groups and other types of consultation are taking place at the same time.

Outcome

Once approved by Command, unit-specific recommendations will be implemented at our division and validated at other divisions. An evaluation process, along with both the implementation, and communication strategies, will be contained within the final report, which is anticipated in the third quarter of 2007.

Please join me in welcoming the team to our division. I am confident you will support the review and give the team your full cooperation.

Michael Federico
Staff Superintendent
X Division

The following three memos are requests for volunteers. Note the different approaches taken. The third memo, written in response to inadequate numbers of volunteers, is "to be read on parade [i.e., at the daily briefing] and posted." Consider the difference in tone in that memo from the other two.

Internal Correspondence

TO:	All Members 52 Division	FROM:	Superintendent Unit Commander, xx Division
		DATE:	2007/06/22

RE: Heart and Stroke Foundation "Big Bike" fundraising event

One in three deaths in Canada every year is due to heart disease and stroke. As police officers, we unfortunately witness these untimely deaths far too often.

Background

The Heart and Stroke Foundation in partnership with Steelback Brewery is hosting the 2007 "Big Bike" races on July 3rd, 2007. This is the same week as the Steelback Grand Prix of Toronto. The "Big Bike" races will take place on the grounds of the Canadian National Exhibition (C.N.E.), running on the same track as the Grand Prix vehicles, although not at the same time.

Event

Teams of thirty will be given the opportunity to race the "Big Bike" once around the track in a race against the clock. Team members are encouraged to seek out sponsors to raise funds to support heart and stroke research.

All participants will receive a pair of three-day general admission passes to the Steelback Grand Prix of Toronto on July 6, 7, & 8.

The winning team will all receive pit area passes for the Steelback Grand Prix of Toronto. The top fundraiser on each team will receive a pair of Gold Grand Prix tickets valued at $400.00. The top overall fundraiser will receive a pair of Grand Prix Pit Lane Suite tickets valued at $2,000.00. All donations over $10.00 are eligible for an official tax receipt.

Funds raised through the "Big Bike" event will fund continued world-class research that saves lives.

All members of xx Division are encouraged to participate in this worthy fundraising event.

For more information, application forms, and sponsor forms, please contact Sergeant Sue Mills #2241 xx Division Community Response, at (416) 444-4444 before June 30th, 2007.

Internal Correspondence

To: All Unit   From: Inspector Debra Preston
     Commanders   Training Unit
                        Date: 2007/06/15

Re: Volunteer Opportunities at Conference

The Saskatchewan Association of Police Training Officers (SAPTO) will hold their 60th annual training conference and trade show in Regina from Friday, September 30, to Monday, October 3, 2007. This conference attracts over 2,000 police leaders from all levels of government, private policing, and educational organizations to discuss mutual challenges and identify solutions. These challenges include recruitment and selection, labour relations issues, and maximizing human resources. The theme of this year's conference is Training the 21st-Century Police Officer.

For a conference of this size to be successful, we require 200 volunteers to assist in a variety of functions. These functions include hospitality, transportation, tourism, information booths, companion programs, trade show exhibits, and security. Volunteers will be provided with job-specific training, uniforms, and meals while working. While off duty, volunteers are encouraged to attend the training sessions and trade show exhibits. An appreciation event will be held post-conference to thank our volunteers for their assistance.

Volunteers needed; possible duties and benefits

Please discuss this event with your members and encourage their participation. For further information on volunteer opportunities and shift availability, please contact Sergeant L. Valentino, volunteer coordinator, at local 8-2212.

Request and contact info

Thank you for your support.

Debra Preston
Inspector
Training Unit

Source: Courtesy of Debra Preston.

Internal Correspondence
TPS 649 1998/011

TO: All Members   FROM: E. Witty
     Communications   Staff Inspector
     Centre   Communications
                                 Centre
                          DATE: 2007/06/19

RE: Staffing Needs for Caribana Weekend

To be read on parade and posted

As you are aware, the 40th annual Caribana Festival Week will take place from Monday, 2007 July 30, to Monday, 2007 August 06. Traditionally Communications

Background

has been able to provide the required staffing for this event utilizing on-duty members augmented by members on call-backs or overtime. The staffing model being used this year to deploy Uniform personnel in the field has required additional personnel from Communications to be assigned to the event.

Problem and possible non-desirable solution

A request for volunteers to work this event has been circulated and some members have volunteered. However, the required staffing level has still not been met and therefore alternative arrangements may have to be made to meet the required staffing. These alternatives may require placing affected members on 12-hour shifts for the event and redeploying members from one shift to either of the other two to provide adequate staffing, or they may require that members' days off be changed to provide the required staffing. The Collective Agreement provides for these alternate schedules upon provision of adequate notice.

Request for volunteers

In order to avoid having to alter shifts or days off, I am encouraging members who are not scheduled to work to consider volunteering to fill the identified vacancies. Communications has canvassed and obtained assistance from members of Communications

Consequences

Support to fill some vacancies. If the required number of vacancies are not filled by June 25, 2007, the Unit Commander of Communications Centre will be required to consider alternatives and may invoke the provisions of the Collective Agreement, which could result in compelling members to work 12-hours shifts or have their days off rescheduled.

Request repeated

I would again ask all members to review their availability to assist during this event.

E. Witty
Staff Inspector
Communications Centre

Source: Courtesy of Superintendent Earl Witty, Toronto Police Service.

As you can see from the above three memos, the typical structure for a memo requesting volunteers is the announcement of the request, details (usually including benefits of volunteering), and a close that gives a deadline and contact information. The last memo, being a second request, is somewhat different. Instead of benefits, it details possible consequences if an adequate number of volunteers do not come forward. It is a nice illustration of realistic consequences rather than an idle threat. The writer refers to the Collective Agreement, the union–management document that governs unionized members' working arrangements. The Collective Agreement allows the alternatives this manager is considering, so he is giving the readers a realistic idea of possible consequences in order to encourage volunteers to come forward. Note the tone. He is not threatening them; he is simply being clear that given the context he may have no choice but to take these steps.

The Explorations for this chapter are less complicated that the situations presented in the examples. For each Exploration, consider the situation and determine your strategy before writing the memo.

EXPLORATIONS

5.1 You had submitted your annual vacation request form to your supervisor when it was due on January 2. It's now March, and you have just got a call from your best friend from college. She or he is getting married. Your friend has a tendency to be spontaneous, and the wedding is in three weeks—at a resort in the Dominican Republic. You have been asked to be best man or maid of honour. You really want to go (and stay a week, if possible). Ask your supervisor for a change of vacation time.

5.2 You have been asked by your supervisor to arrange and conduct a meeting to discuss expanding to other divisions a program you initiated at a local school to keep students off drugs. Send a memo announcing the meeting.

5.3 You would like to attend a series of workshops being jointly sponsored by your police service and the local university's Justice Studies program. Attendance is free, but participants must be recommended by their supervisor. Write a memo to your supervisor stating your interest in attending.

5.4 You recently attended a conference in the United States where the Sarasota County Sheriff presented his department's Internet arrest card program as a means of crime deterrence (see www.sarasotasheriff.org/arrests.asp). Write a memo suggesting to your supervisor that such a program be tried in your jurisdiction.

5.5 You are the supervisor who has received the suggestion in Exploration 5.4. Respond to the suggestion.

5.6 Your department is instituting a policy change and requiring all uniformed officers to wear Kevlar vests when on duty. Write a memo announcing the policy change, including letting officers know how to get fitted for the vests.

5.7 Report to your unit commander on a public meeting that had been sponsored jointly by your division and the community liaison committee.

5.8 Write a memo reminding your division of the policy and/or procedures regarding proper use of notebooks.

5.9 Write a memo announcing a mandatory workshop on recent court decisions regarding searches.

5.10 Write a memo reminding officers to sign up for the annual use-of-force training.

5.11 Write a memo to your unit commander suggesting that bicycle patrols be expanded in your division.

5.12 Write a memo announcing workshops on guidelines for TASER use.

5.13 Write a memo to your unit commander informing him or her about the results of a recent traffic enforcement blitz.

5.14 Write a memo looking for volunteers to sit on Program Advisory Committees for Police Foundation/Law Enforcement programs at area colleges.

Chapter 6

Communicating with the Public: Letters

As we saw in the last chapter, memorandums (or memos) are sent within the organization. Letters are used to communicate with those outside the organization. Community policing or community mobilization is an important part of law enforcement strategy today. Community policing aims to break down barriers between the police and the people they serve. Connecting with the public is therefore very important. As noted in an earlier chapter, this is sometimes done by putting police officers in the community on either foot or bicycle patrol. It is accomplished by meeting with people in a community setting at times other than when a crime has been committed. The public is seen as partnering with police, not only in solving crimes (through efforts such as Crime Stoppers or other "tip lines"), but also in preventing crime and improving the quality of life for all. Those in the community are invited to join with the police in seeking solutions to community problems.

A Note on Letter Format

Let's look at letter format before we look at several examples. Standard letter format is as follows:

```
Sender's address (or police service letterhead)

Date

Receiver's name and address

Salutation (Dear …):

Text of letter single-spaced at margin; line left
blank between paragraphs

Complimentary close (Sincerely; Yours truly)

Signature

Sender's name printed below signature

Sender's position
```

The following letter is an example of an effort to make a connection. (With two exceptions, noted below, the letters in this chapter, as with the memos in Chapter 5, were written by students who are practising police officers).

```
                    Toronto Police Service
                       555 Bloor Street
                       Toronto, Ontario
                    www.torontopolice.on.ca

June 19, 2007

Joel Gorenkoff, Principal
North Toronto Collegiate
70 Roehampton Avenue
Toronto, Ontario
M5J 3L3

Dear Principal Gorenkoff:

Subject: 2007—2008 Police/School Administrator
         Orientation Session

The Toronto Police Service, in partnership with the   Invitation
Toronto District School Board and the Toronto
Catholic School Board, is hosting the 2007—2008
Police/School Administrator Orientation Session. I
```

am pleased to invite you to attend this year's event, which will be held at St. Basil the Great College School on Wednesday, August 29, 2007, from 8:00 a.m. to 1:00 p.m.

The safety of the students and staff in our community schools is of paramount importance to all of us. Youth violence in the City of Toronto occurs in neighbourhoods, plazas, recreational facilities, and, unfortunately, in our schools. A school environment that is free of violence and threats of violence is one in which our children can learn, grow, and thrive. The Toronto Police Service is committed to assisting you and your staff to provide that safe environment.

Details

The Police/School Administrator Orientation Session will include school administrators from all Toronto high schools and the police officers assigned to those schools. The session will allow all of us to exchange ideas and revisit police/school protocols so that we all have a better understanding of each other's roles in helping to create a safe school environment.

Request for RSVP

Please RSVP with your name or that of a designate before the end of the 2006—2007 school year to: Detective Harold Addams by phone at 416-808-5351 or by e-mail—Harold.Addams@torontopolice.on.ca

Compli- mentary close

I have attached an agenda describing the events scheduled for the day. I look forward to meeting with you and moving forward with our shared goals and objectives to create safe schools for all involved.

Yours truly,

Brian F. O'Connor
Inspector
Toronto Police Service
Enclosure

Source: Courtesy of Brian O'Connor.

In another example, a member of the community is thanked for participating in a community summit meeting on violence in one of Canada's major cities.

Police Service
Community Road
Toronto, Ontario
M6S 3B5

October 19, 2008

Ms. Kathy Hunt
855 Don Mills Road #3403
Toronto, Ontario
M3C 1V9

Dear Ms. Hunt:

Recent violent occurrences in Toronto have raised significant concerns throughout the community among police, politicians, media, and the general public about how we can ensure that our streets remain safe and protect our citizens from being victims of violent crime.

Background

The Summit entitled "Rallying Toronto Against Violence," held Tuesday May 30, and Wednesday, May 31, 2007, permitted the Toronto Police Service and the Province of Ontario to work with appropriate stakeholders to devise and implement solutions to this serious problem.

Event

I would like to thank you for your support and participation in this Summit. Only through the involvement of people with a stake in the problem of street violence and a role to play in finding solutions could the Summit achieve its goal of developing concrete solutions to violence on Toronto's streets.

Thank you

I particularly enjoyed our conversation during the lunch break Tuesday afternoon. Your concerns regarding the graffiti in South Park have been passed on to the 33 Division Community Response Unit. Sergeant John Smith will be in contact with you to discuss your concerns.

Personal note

"Rallying Toronto Against Violence" was one of a number of symposia taking place early in 2007, but is the only one that focused on the implementation of practical solutions. Given the current fiscal climate and the urgency of the situation, it was essential that the solutions be capable of being implemented with minimal delay and expense.

Importance

I look forward to our continued partnership in implementing the solutions identified during the Summit.

Sincerely,

Philip Heath
Staff Sergeant
Police Service
xx Division

Partnering with the community also involves learning from experts in fields other than policing. The next letter is an example of an invitation to such an expert.

Police Service
Community Road
Toronto, Ontario
M6S 3B5

June 25th, 2007

Mr. Dave Franklin
Domestic Violence Consultant
100 Maple Street
Toronto, Ontario   M5V 3C6

Dear Mr. Franklin:

I would like to invite you to speak at the next 24-7 Lecture being held on September 10th, 2007.

The 24-7 Lecture is an innovative lecture series that is held twice a year in the auditorium of Police Headquarters located at 40 College Street. The lecture involves the participation of twenty-four different speakers, who are given seven minutes each to present their topic. The fast-paced concept has been proven to provide a wide variety of important topics in a short period of time. There is a signal given at six minutes, and a buzzer will sound at the completion of seven minutes. You will be provided an exact time for your presentation two weeks prior to the lecture.

The live audience is comprised of approximately one hundred police supervisors from all areas of the Toronto Police Service. The lecture is also taped and distributed to all officers through a video link on our internal computer system. Officers will be able to view the lecture at any time during their shift.

The theme for this 24-7 Lecture will be Domestic Violence. The speakers will include experts from the medical field, legal field, social services, and police officers. I am requesting that you speak about Relationship Terrorism.

Specific request

Please advise if you would be able to participate in this lecture. Your contribution would be appreciated. Should you have any questions about this lecture, please feel free to contact me at 416-808-4876.

RSVP and contact info

Sincerely,

Cory Bockus
D/Sgt. #5648

Source: Courtesy of Cory Bockus.

As mentioned briefly in the last chapter, there are two approaches in organizing either a letter or a memo. The writer can use either a direct or an indirect approach. A *direct* approach is used when the audience for the communication will be positive or indifferent about what you are writing. An *indirect* approach is used when the audience response will likely not be favourable (you're delivering bad news), or if the reader must be persuaded (as with a request or suggestion). While the direct approach is usually used in memos in policing organizations, when communicating outside the organization a writer must consider whether to use a direct or an indirect approach. (Members of the public have not taken an oath to follow orders!)

Let's look at the two approaches. The following letters were written by Police Foundations students. The first uses a direct approach. With a direct approach, you get to the point immediately: open with what you want (the letter's purpose), give necessary details, then close with next steps (what you want the reader to do).

```
            Father John Redmond Secondary School
                    30 Valermo Drive
                    Toronto, Ontario
                       M8Z 1Y4
                     416-253-1234

February 3, 2007

Constable Jerry Brown
51 Division
Toronto Police Service
3 Jane Street
Toronto, Ontario
M2K 1P3

Dear Constable Brown:
```

Invitation

I am the President of Father John Redmond Parent Council, and I would like to invite you to speak at our March School Council meeting.

The School Council meeting will focus on a discussion of whether we should begin a peer mediation program at our school. Other schools with peer mediation programs have recommended we have you in to speak about setting up a peer mediation program.

Details

```
Date:        March 15, 2007
Time:        7:30 p.m.
Location:    Father John Redmond School cafeteria
             30 Valermo Drive
```

Could you address an audience of about 30–35 parents on your experiences setting up peer mediation programs? We are especially interested in hearing about

• the process for setting up a program

• the challenges of running a program

• the results programs have shown

The presentation should be approximately 15 minutes, with a further 15 minutes for questions.

Please let me know by February 25 if you'll be able to address our group, so I can advertise your presentation. Thank you. RSVP

Sincerely,

Lucy Valentino
President
Father John Redmond School Council

The class assumed that the reader, Constable Brown, would be positively disposed toward the request, since he is a Community Liaison Officer, someone whose job it is to make connections with the public. They therefore chose the direct approach. Constable Brown's reply would either use the direct approach, if he's able to accept the invitation, or the indirect approach, if he's unable to attend the meeting. Here is an example of the former, again student-generated, followed by the negative response. Note the differences in how the two letters are structured.

Toronto Police Service
51 Division
3 Jane Street
Toronto, Ontario
M2K 1P3

February 7, 2007

Lucy Valentino
President, School Council
Father John Redmond High School
30 Valermo Drive
Toronto, Ontario
M8Z 1Y4

Dear Ms. Valentino:

Thank you for the invitation to address your March meeting. I'd be happy to accept. I'd like to confirm the details of the presentation:

Date: March 15, 2007
Time: 7:30 p.m.
Location: Father John Redmond High School Cafeteria
            30 Valermo Drive

Direct approach: accept and confirm details

I'll deliver a 15-minute presentation on peer mediation programs to an audience of 30–35 parents, with 15 minutes for questions. I will cover:

- the process for setting up a peer mediation program
- the challenges of running a program
- the results of programs I've helped set up

Require-
mentsI will require a VCR and monitor for the presentation. I have enclosed a copy of the handout I'll be distributing that night. I'll be bringing 40 copies; please let me know if more will be needed.

ContactIf you need to contact me, please call me at 416-274-7788, ext 421, or email me at jbrown@mtpd.com. Once again, thanks for your invitation. I look forward to working with your group.

Sincerely,

Jerry Brown
Toronto Police Service
Enclosure

Toronto Police Service
51 Division
3 Jane Street
Toronto, Ontario
M2K 1P3

February 7, 2007

Lucy Valentino
President, School Council
Father John Redmond High School
22 Valermo Drive
Toronto, Ontario
M8Z 1Y4

Dear Ms. Valentino:

Indirect
opening
showing
point of
agreementThank you for your invitation to speak about Peer Mediation Programs at your March School Council meeting. Peer mediation programs are an effective way to decrease violence in schools and help students learn strategies for conflict resolution.

Communicating with the Public: Letters **127**

Unfortunately, I have another speaking engagement on March 15. I'd like to present two alternatives:

1. Constable Fred Jones could address your group in my place. Constable Jones has worked with me on a number of peer mediation projects.

2. I am available to speak at your April meeting, if the talk can be rescheduled.

Please let me know if either option works for your group and if so, which you prefer. We look forward to helping your group decide if a peer mediation program is right for your school.

If you would like to contact me by phone, I can be reached at 416-323-4927, ext. 3216 between 9:00 a.m. and 6:00 p.m. most days, or by e-mail at jbrown@mtpd.com. I look forward to hearing from you.

Sincerely,

Jerry Brown
Toronto Police Service

Declines, but offers alternatives

Switch from "I" to "we." Why?

Contact info

An indirect approach builds to the main point. In this second example, Constable Brown begins by thanking the group for the invitation, and acknowledging the importance of the topic. He moves on to give the bad news that he is unavailable to speak, but offers positive options, and closes in a forward-looking way.

In all of these examples, note the use of bulleted and/or numbered lists to make the ideas easier for the reader to grasp. In memo and letter writing, you want to use reader-friendly prose. Think about using bulleted or numbered lists, italics and bolding, or even subheadings to help the reader catch your message easily.

Serving the public also involves being accountable; communication outside the organization will therefore include responding to public complaints. The following three letters are responses to complaints. Note the tone of the letters, and the care the writers take to make sure the reader feels that he or she has been taken seriously and that the complaint has been investigated fairly.

The Guelph Humber Police Service
Part Time Justice Studies Division
www.justice.open.uoguelph.ca

July 17, 2007

Mr. C. A. Complainant
123 Any Street
Toronto ON, M5L 6T9

Dear Mr. Complainant:

Details of complaint

Thank you for your letter of June 12. In your correspondence you raise two issues: first you ask that a sign be posted on southbound Jane Street, approaching Eglinton Avenue, that clearly indicates the speed limit is 50 km/h. Second, you question the competence of Police Constable Goodofficer to enforce the speed limit using a speed-measuring device.

I will deal with your questions in order.

Response to 1st issue

1) The Highway Traffic Act, the statute that governs the operation of motor vehicles in the province of Ontario, stipulates:

   No person shall drive a motor vehicle at a rate of speed greater than 50 kilometres per hour on a highway within a local municipality or within a built-up area (ss. 128(1)).

This subsection means that, unless otherwise posted, the speed limit in municipalities in Ontario is 50 km/h. Accordingly, where no signs are posted, the speed limit within the City of Toronto is 50 km/h. Therefore, it is not necessary for the City to post a sign on Jane Street in the area where you were driving—the warning sign you note in your letter is adequate notice to alert drivers that the speed limit changes from 60 km/h to 50 km/h.

Response to 2nd issue

2) Constable Goodofficer is a traffic specialist at X Division who is qualified to enforce the speed limit laws through the use of speed-measuring devices. I am confident Constable Goodofficer is competent, and is responsibly fulfilling his duties. However, motorists charged with speeding by officers who have used such devices may challenge the officer's training and skills in court when their case is heard. If you wish to contest this matter in court, please follow the instructions on the summons you received from Constable Goodofficer.

I trust this information is helpful. Thank you for bringing this matter to my attention and giving me an opportunity to respond.

Courteous close

Yours truly,

Mike Federico
Staff Superintendent

Source: Courtesy of Michael Federico.

Police Service
Community Road
Toronto, Ontario
M6S 3B5

July 21, 2007

Ms. Mary Smith
123 Elm Street
Owen Sound, Ontario
A1A 1A1

Dear Ms Smith:

I am in receipt of your letter of complaint dated January 1, 2007. Please be assured that the Toronto Police Service is very concerned with the safety of all persons, resident or visitor, enjoying the numerous activities offered by the various venues within the City of Toronto.

Indirect opening showing empathy

I was disheartened to hear of your unfortunate encounter with the unruly fans as you exited the Rogers Centre following the Blue Jays game on the evening of July 17, 2007.

I share your concern that despite repeated calls to 911 you did not have a uniformed officer respond for 15 minutes and unfortunately several minutes after the suspect(s) had roughed you up and disappeared into the crowd.

I immediately ordered an investigation to be conducted into the matter by Staff Sergeant Joe Blow of the Communications Centre. Our investigation, a copy of which you shall receive in the mail in due

What was done, what was learned: details

course, shows that there were fifty paid duty officers on duty that night. These officers are retained by the venue organizers and are responsible for security within the building itself, not the surrounding public streets. I understand from your correspondence that the incident to which you refer occurred one block north of the Rogers Centre.

The division of responsibility for the area of the Rogers Centre, 52 Division, had twenty-eight officers on duty at the time of the incident. Our records indicate that all the divisional officers were engaged in calls for service that had a higher designated priority level than your incident.

Tactful conclusion

A review of our policy and procedures show our personnel followed Service-directed guidelines in this matter. It is unfortunate that our police service cannot be everywhere at all times to prevent crime. I am glad to see you were not injured. I hope your future visits to our city are more pleasant and incident-free.

Sincerely,

Staff Inspector Hammer
Police Service
Professional Standards—Complaints

Source: Courtesy of D/Sgt Art Little, #935 Professional Standards.

Toronto Police Service
Mounted and Police Dog Services
40 College Street
Toronto, Ontario M5J 2J3

June 20, 2007

Mr. Michael Smith
50 College Street
Toronto, Ontario M5J 2J5

Dear Mr. Smith:

Indirect opening, paraphrasing issues

Thank you for your letter of June 18th, 2007. I appreciate that you are concerned about the horse manure left on the street by police mounted patrols.

I also understand that you feel the police should be as accountable as dog owners when it comes to cleaning up after their animals.

The duties performed by our officers on horseback make it difficult to clean up the manure after the horses defecate. Dismounting from the horse reduces the control the rider has, and this can put the officer, horse, and community at risk.

<aside>Reasons for problem</aside>

Horses are grazing animals and their digestive systems are continually engaged in processing food. They pass the waste material four to five times a day and there is no way the rider can regulate where or when the manure will pass. The fact that horses are herbivores means that the manure will break down much quickly than the manure from carnivorous animals such as dogs. Generally, horse manure will have broken down and disintegrated within 24 to 48 hours of being deposited.

<aside>Clarification of situation: not a health issue</aside>

Being herbivores also means there is no toxicity or disease associated with horse manure. In fact, many carnivorous animals will eat the manure for the proteins it contains.

Our horses are exempt from all City bylaws. The officers are not committing any infractions when the manure is not cleaned up. Our officers avoid riding on the sidewalks, foot paths, and bicycle paths when possible in order to avoid leaving manure in places where people have to walk or cycle. On occasion, horses will defecate in these areas, and when that happens the officers will dismount if it is safe and remove the manure. If it is not possible for the officer to remove the manure and they feel it poses a hazard to the public, they will call for a City works crew to have the manure removed.

<aside>Policy details</aside>

In conclusion, if our horses defecate on the street, it will be left to degrade or to be cleaned by City street sweepers. If the manure is on the sidewalk or a pathway, we will arrange to have it removed. The Toronto Police Service is dedicated to working with the community. We are responsive to complaints about the service we provide. If you wish to discuss this issue further please telephone me directly at (416) 808—1713.

<aside>Conclusion and intact info</aside>

If at any time you are concerned that one of our horses has defecated in an area that poses a risk or a hazard to the public, please telephone the Mounted Unit Supervisor at (416) 808—1719. The supervisor will investigate your complaint and, if necessary, have the manure removed.

Sincerely,

Bill Wardle
Staff Inspector
Mounted and Police Dog Services

Source: Courtesy of William Wardle.

Letters will also need to be written in response to requests. The following letter responds to a request for information about summer jobs.

Police Service
Community Road
Toronto, Ontario
M6S 3B5

June 19, 2007

Mr. Geoffrey Howard
323 Johnston Avenue
Whitby, Ontario L9R 3S4

Dear Mr. Howard:

Indirect: paraphrase of request

I am in receipt of your letter dated June 1, 2007, to Chief William Blair, enquiring about summer student positions with the Toronto Police Service. I understand that you are a third-year Psychology student at the University of Toronto and have a particular interest in the field of Criminal Psychology.

Details re: unit

The Toronto Police Service, Behavioural Assessment Section, is part of the Sex Crimes Unit. This section conducts threat assessments and monitors offenders designated as high risk to re-offend. Officers assigned to this section receive training in the area of criminal psychology and behavioural analysis, and frequently work with Criminal Psychologists.

While I am quite interested in your proposed research project, as noted in your letter of introduction, I must advise that all summer employment opportunities are provided through the Service's Human Resource Unit. As such I have forwarded your résumé and references to Ms. Marilyn Jones, coordinator of the employment program. She will be in contact with you in the near future.

Expression of interest, what was done (following procedures)

Should you have any questions about the hiring process, please contact Ms. Jones directly at (416) 808-7643. If you would like additional information about the Toronto Police Service Behavioural Assessment Section, contact Detective Sergeant Bill Davis at (416) 808-7447.

Contact info

Thank you for your interest in employment with the Service and good luck as you continue with your education.

Courteous close

Sincerely,

Frances Smith
Inspector, Sex Crimes Unit

Source: Courtesy of Elizabeth Byrnes.

EXPLORATIONS

For some of the following Explorations, you might want to check out police service websites for additional information on the specific topic of the letter.

6.1 You are the director of Seniors First, a community program for seniors in your area. Invite the police service Community Liaison Officer for your area to present a talk on personal safety for seniors.

6.2 You are a Community Liaison Officer. You have been invited by the director of Seniors First, a community program for seniors in the area, to present a talk on personal safety for seniors. Accept the invitation.

6.3 You are a Community Liaison Officer. You have been invited by the director of Seniors First, a community program for seniors in the area to present a talk on personal safety for seniors. You are not able to accept the invitation. Offer alternatives.

6.4 You are a graduate of your school's Police Foundations Program (PFP), and a police service staff sergeant. You have been invited to join the PFP Advisory Committee. Accept the invitation.

6.5 You are a graduate of your school's Police Foundations Program (PFP), and a police service staff sergeant. You have been invited to join the PFP Advisory Committee. Decline the invitation. Offer alternatives.

6.6 You are a staff sergeant. You have received a citizen complaint regarding her treatment by one of your constables when she was stopped for driving under the influence. Respond to the complaint.

6.7 You are a senior officer in a police service. You have received a letter from a citizen with a suggestion. The citizen was vacationing in Sarasota County, Florida, and heard about the Sarasota County Internet Arrest Card program (see http://sarasotasheriff.org/arrests.asp). The citizen thinks your police service should try such a program as a crime deterrent. Respond to the citizen's suggestion.

6.8 Your senior officer has received a letter from a citizen with a suggestion. The citizen was vacationing in Sarasota County, Florida, and heard about the Sarasota County Internet Arrest Card program (see http://sarasotasheriff.org/arrests.asp). The citizen thinks your police service should try such a program as a crime deterrent. Your senior officer has asked you to get more information about the program. Write a letter to the Sarasota County Sheriff's Department requesting specific information that will be useful to your senior officer.

6.9 You plan to attend a provincial policing conference next November. Write a letter to the conference organizer with suggestions of workshop topics you would like to see included in the conference.

6.10 You are a ten-year veteran of a Canadian police service. You are interested in criminal profiling. You are considering taking a leave of absence to pursue training in this area. Write a letter to the FBI Academy in Quantico, Maryland, asking for information about their profiling training.

6.11 You are in the community mobilization unit in your division. Write a letter to students in social and community service programs in area colleges, encouraging them to volunteer to sit on your division's Community Liaison Committee.

6.12 As a practising police officer, you have received a letter from a local college's Police Foundations Program asking for your thoughts on what knowledge and skills are needed to be successful in your police service.

6.13 You are coordinator of your college's Policing Day, an annual event where practising law enforcement professionals meet with students in your Police Foundations Program. The highlight of the day is a panel presentation by senior members/executives of the police force(s) in your geographical area. Write a letter inviting the chief of police to be a part of the panel.

6.14 You are the chief of police who received the invitation in Exploration 6.13. Accept the invitation.

6.15 You are the chief of police who received the invitation in Exploration 6.13. Decline the invitation, but give alternatives.

6.16 Use information from a police service website to write a letter to a relevant group informing them about how to prevent a specific crime, such as identity theft or break and enter.

6.17 Write a letter to local businesses announcing the parking strategy outlined in the memo found on page 100 in Chapter 5.

6.18 Respond to a complaint regarding a ticket received under the parking strategy outlined in the memo found on page 100 in Chapter 5.

6.19 Write a letter announcing a graffiti cleanup campaign, and ask for volunteers from the community to participate.

Chapter 7

Communicating with the Public: Brochures and Flyers

Community policing rests on a police service's ability to connect with the public. Much of that connection is face-to-face, with uniform officers returning to the streets from their former paperwork prisons. Some of that connection, especially in terms of providing information so that people can protect themselves, is achieved through brochures and flyers. The emerging field of social marketing aims to harness the power of marketing, including Internet marketing, to influence individuals' behaviour to improve their well-being and that of society (www.social-marketing.org/aboutus.html). Police officers don't tend to think of themselves as marketers, but that is what they must sometimes be if they are to reach the public, especially vulnerable groups, so that all can participate in their own safekeeping.

Brochures, distributed in hard copy and also available electronically via a police srvice website, can help prevent seniors from falling prey to identify theft, educate homeowners on how to protect themselves from theft through simple environmental design changes, help neighbourhoods to come together to eradicate graffiti, or provide important information about a current community issue such as marijuana grow houses or high-end auto theft. Flyers posted throughout a neighbourhood can invite citizens to a community meeting, or encourage them to be part of a police–community liaison committee.

The process of marketing in policing can be learned, and it can be enjoyable. It is important to remember that what you are doing is advertising, and *advertising* is primarily a *visual medium*. It is essential that whatever brochures or flyers you produce be attractive visually and be pleasing to the eye.

Brochures and Flyers

What's the difference between a brochure and a flyer? A flyer, as I'm using the term, is a single sheet of paper, often meant to be posted, and always meant to attract attention and to convey a message almost instantaneously. A brochure might also be just one sheet of paper, but it is folded, contains more information, and takes a bit longer to read. Brochures for police services are sometimes produced professionally, but division staff can also create brochures themselves. The following are not the only styles of brochure, but they are probably the easiest:

- 8 1/2" × 11" sheet folded in half
- 8 1/2" × 14" sheet folded in three, with two ends meeting in the middle
- 8 1/2" × 11" sheet folded in even thirds, the first third folded to the right, and the last third folded to the middle, under the first

To see how each is folded, take a look at Figure 7.1.

Writing Copy

You have chosen the third type of brochure style. Now you need to write your copy (compose the text of the brochure). Actually, you would never really think of the text separately;

Figure 7.1

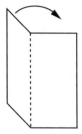 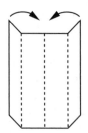 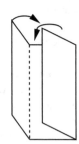

you must always consider, at the same time, how your ad will look. However, for the sake of simplicity let's talk just about text, or copy, for now.

You can't say everything. A good ad is an economical one—economical not just in terms of getting the most for your money, but also in getting the most for your words. Choose what is most important. What do you most want to tell people about your topic?

With a brochure, you must capture readers' attention, tell them a few significant things, and then let them go. In selecting what to put in the brochure, consider it from the reader's point of view: Does the reader really want or need to know this particular information? If yes, fine; otherwise, leave it out.

As you write, keep in mind the literacy level of your target audience. Don't be patronizing in your language, but remember that some of your readers may be functionally illiterate, or might have English as a second language. (Many services translate important brochures into several languages.) Write clearly, simply, and concisely.

Let's assume you have identified a potential problem with 911 use in your city. If someone calls 911 from a landline home phone, the 911 Communications Centre automatically has the phone owner's name, address, and so on, so help can be dispatched to an exact location. If the call is from a cell phone, the Communications Centre can tell the location of the nearest cell phone tower to the caller (in a major city, about a 3-km range). Help can therefore only be dispatched to an exact location if the caller can say where she or he is. Finally, if the caller has voice over Internet service (VOIP), no location information whatsoever is transmitted to the Communications Centre.

You want to be sure citizens are aware of these realities, so they can use the 911 service effectively. The text of your brochure (the copy) will focus on what information the Communications Centre gets automatically in a 911 call from the different types of phone services.

Designing a Brochure

With the style of brochure you have chosen, you have six usable surfaces:

- Page 1, actually the last third of the back of the sheet
- Pages 2 through 4, each a third of the front of the sheet
- Pages 5 and 6, the other two-thirds of the back of the sheet

Confused? Get out a sheet of paper, turn it 90 degrees, fold the last third to the left, then the first third to the right. Number the pages as indicated above.

On page 1 you want the *headline*, something to catch the reader's attention. Pages 2 through 4 could describe what information the Communications Centre gets from each type of phone service. Page 5 (which would be seen second) could give information about the Communications Centre and 911 calls, and page 6 could give contact information.

Figure 7.2 shows how the brochure might look.

Figure 7.2

911

Help emergency personnel find you

Know your location

Want more information?

Contact us!

Communications Centre

Your Police Department

905-833-5543

www.ypd.ca

In an emergency

911

Help us find you!

Figure 7.2 (continued)

Did you know?

Different types of phone services give 911 operators different information?

Calls from a standard land-line (house) phone provide:

• Name of owner
• Street address

Calls from a cell phone provide:

• The closest phone tower

• In most cities, that means 5 to 15 km

• In some locations, it might even be 30 km

• A lot of ground to search!

Calls from VOIP (Internet phone service) provide:

• No location info at all

• So where do we start?

Help us help you —Always know where you are

Designing a Flyer

As I mentioned, a flyer is designed for quick visual impact. With today's word-processing programs, it's easy to design a flyer. Because you might want to photocopy the flyer, you would not use colour (way too expensive!) but instead use different fonts and text box features to achieve visual impact.

Figure 7.3 shows an example of a flyer.

Here are a few hints for designing your own flyer:

• For visual interest, use *contrast*—different type sizes, different lines (diagonals, horizontals, verticals). Compose your ad as you would a painting.

• Remember that English-speakers read from left to right, and from top to bottom; ensure that the order of the text or illustrations works with this natural reading tendency.

- Be sure to leave plenty of white space (space where there is neither text nor illustration); the eye becomes fatigued if a page is too "busy" and if there is no white space for the eye to rest. But watch out for too much white space—it will look as though you have nothing to say!

Figure 7.3

EXPLORATIONS

7.1 Explore some police service websites looking for informational brochures.

7.2 Create a flyer to advertise a community information meeting.

7.3 Prepare a brochure on your division's community police liaison committee. Include the information on the committee that would be most helpful, including how to join the committee.

7.4 Create a brochure on one of the following topics (do an Internet search for any information needed):

- Auto Theft Prevention
- Preventing Identity Theft
- Safe Internet Use (audience: children and/or teenagers)
- Crime Prevention through Environmental Design
- Domestic Abuse
- Graffiti Prevention
- Marijuana Grow Houses

7.5 Go to the "Papers" section of the Social Marketing Institute Website (www.social-marketing.org/papers.html) and read the Conference Proceedings of the 2000 Marketing Summit Conference to gain insight into social marketing.

Chapter 8

Using Graphics in Workplace Writing: Basic Types of Graphics and When to Use Them

In reports and presentations, we often use graphics to illustrate a point succinctly. This chapter discusses when and how to use graphics, describes different types of graphics, and provides examples of some different types.

What Are Graphics?

A graphic is any illustration in a report or presentation. You probably are familiar with several types of graphics, such as tables, bar charts, pie charts, line charts or graphs, photos, and cartoons. We will be discussing only the mathematical types of graphics.

Why Use Graphics?

Graphics are used to communicate information efficiently. Graphics can convey a quick visual impression to make a point quickly, or provide detailed information in an easy-to-understand format.

When Do I Use Graphics?

Graphics are used to communicate information efficiently. They are used for a purpose. If you have a fancy graphics program on your computer, you may be tempted to overuse graphics. But graphics should be used only if they are relevant to your report or presentation. They must *add* to your communication, not distract the audience's attention from your main point. So as you write, or as you prepare a presentation, ask yourself if a graphic will help you to convey your message. If a graphic would merely be a frill, leave it out.

How Do I Use Graphics?

Once you have decided to use a graphic, you are faced with two decisions: which type to use and where to place the graphic. You also need to consider graphics conventions—that is, how to present your graphics in a format that is standard in the business and professional community.

Graphics Conventions

Every graphic must have the following:

- A number. As we'll discuss below, tables are numbered separately from all other graphics. The number makes it easy to refer to the proper graphic in the text of your report or presentation.
- An explanatory title, so the audience knows what the graphic is supposed to show and is prepared to understand it.
- Labels on columns and rows, so the audience can decipher the graphic.
- A unit of measurement, such as dollars, thousands of dollars, hundreds of people, millions of housing units, and so on.
- Any explanatory notes that are necessary to understand the graphic, especially definitions of key terms.
- The source of the graphic, if you did not gather the numbers yourself.

Take a look at the sample graphic below.

Table 8.1

YOUTH CORRECTIONAL SERVICES, ADMISSIONS TO PROVINCIAL AND TERRITORIAL PROGRAMS, BY PROVINCE AND TERRITORY (NEWFOUNDLAND AND LABRADOR)

	2000	2001	2002	2003	2004
			numbers		
N.L. Remand	**211**	**224**	**285**	**159**	**154**
Males	166	178	218	128	126
Females	45	46	67	31	28
Sex unknown	0	0	0	0	0
Aboriginals	12	8	8	7	10
Non-Aboriginals	194	204	187	137	130
Aboriginal identity unknown	5	12	90	15	14
Admissions to secure custody	**183**	**168**	**201**	**86**	**52**
Males	161	148	160	70	44
Females	22	20	41	15	8
Sex unknown	0	0	0	1	0
Aboriginals	13	6	14	5	4
Non-Aboriginals	163	152	150	76	47
Aboriginal identity unknown	7	10	37	5	1
Admissions to open custody	**146**	**152**	**148**	**59**	**64**
Males	125	122	124	47	58
Females	21	30	24	12	6
Sex unknown	0	0	0	0	0
Aboriginals	26	9	17	5	4
Non-Aboriginals	113	139	112	48	60
Aboriginal identity unknown	7	4	19	6	0
			days		
Median time served					
On remand	8	10	7	6	7
In secure custody	30	30	53	45	60
In open custody	90	62	90	60	61
			numbers		
Admissions to probation	**627**	**590**	**490**	**430**	**344**
Males	501	453	392	344	278
Females	126	137	98	79	62
Sex unknown	0	0	0	7	4
					(*continued*)

Table 8.1 (continued)

	2000	2001	2002	2003	2004
Aboriginals	39	30	26	25	12
Non-Aboriginals	560	531	404	379	322
Aboriginal identity unknown	28	29	60	26	10
			days		
Median probation order length	365	365	365	367	365

Note: Fiscal year (April 1 through March 31). Not all variables are applicable to or available for all jurisdictions. Inter-jurisdictional comparisons of the data should be made with caution.
Source: Statistics Canada, "Youth correctional services, admissions to provincial and territorial programs, by province and territory (Newfoundland and Labrador)," http://www40.statcan.ca/l01/cst01/legal42b.htm.

Note the *number*, Table 8.1, which indicates that it is the first table in Chapter 8. Note the *title*, which indicates exactly what the subject of this table is: Youth correctional services, admissions to provincial and territorial programs by province and territory (Newfoundland and Labrador). We know exactly what to expect because of the explanatory title. This graphic will list the admissions to youth correctional services in Newfoundland and Labrador. The *unit of measurement* (number) is also given in the title. We know that this is the exact number of youths (rather than, for example, needing to multiply by 100 if the unit of measurement were given in hundreds). Note the clear use of *labels* on columns and rows. *Notes* are provided to explain that the measurement year was April through March, and that comparisons between provinces should be made with caution. Finally, the *source* indicates exactly where this graphic came from.

Types of Graphics

Of the many types of graphics, I will discuss the following major types: tables, line charts, bar charts, and pie charts. There is a "right" graphic for every communication task. Which one you choose depends on your purpose and on your data.

Tables

Tables, as I have mentioned, are in a class by themselves. They are numbered as tables, whereas all other graphics are numbered as figures or charts (whether you number all the others as figures or number them all charts is up to you, but choose one and be consistent).

Tables present detailed information in an accessible format. They do not make a quick visual impression, but they do allow the reader to extract particular pieces of information. For example, look back at Table 8.1. How many non-Aboriginals were remanded in 2002? How many in 2004? How many females were admitted to open custody in 2005?

Those answers are relatively easy to find. Now let me ask another question, and see how quickly you can answer it. Which type of disposition (remand, admission to open custody, admission to secure custody) declined in 2002? Can you tell me in thirty seconds? Why not?

You could have answered that last question immediately if you were looking at another type of graphic, such as a line chart. Tables are great for providing detailed information. Their limitation is that they require some work on the part of readers. Readers must compare data and make inferences. The advantage, of course, is that the data are there, rich and available for exploration. The drawback is that sometimes, as a writer, you may want to do the readers' thinking for them.

Line Charts

Chances are you learned to do a line chart back in high-school math class. You had an x and a y axis (or ordinate and abscissa, if you want to get fancy), and you were given some values and told to plot the chart. Line charts are appropriate for showing the rise or fall of what is graphed. Look at the line chart in Figure 8.1.

Did the number of deaths go up or down between 2000 and 2005? In which two years was there a surge in birth? What is the trend in births in Canada?

All of these questions are easy to answer by looking at the line chart. If I were to ask you to give me numbers exact to the

Figure 8.1

BIRTHS AND DEATHS

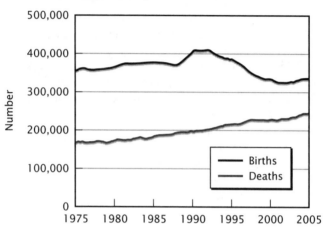

Source: Statistics Canada, "Births and deaths," adapted from the Statistics Canada CANSIM database, Table 051-0004, http://cansim2.statcan.ca.

last digit, however, you would have more difficulty answering. Line charts provide approximations.

Here's a line chart from the Toronto Police Service 2006 Environmental Scan. Has the total number of break and enters in Toronto gone up or down since 1996? In 2004, were there more residential break and enters, or more commercial B and E's?

All of these things are easy to see in Figure 8.2.

Look back at Table 8.1. What sorts of details could you provide from this table that you could not provide from a line chart? What advantage, though, does a line chart have over a table?

A few things to note about line charts: First, keep the number of lines to a minimum. Generally, three or four lines make for readability in a line chart; any more (especially if they intersect), and the chart looks like a nest of snakes—and who wants to get involved with a nest of snakes? The other important thing to note about line charts is the way one line is differentiated from another. *Differentiate by weight, not by colour.*

Figure 8.2

NUMBER OF BREAK AND ENTERS

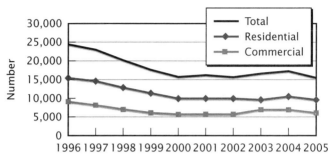

Source: *Environmental Scan 2006*, Toronto Police Service.

By this I mean draw one line as a series of dots, one as dashes, and so on, or vary the thickness or density of grey, rather than making one line blue, one green, and so on. With the spread of colour photocopiers, this piece of advice may soon be dated, but currently, when reports are copied, they are generally copied on a standard black-and-white photocopier. So what happens to all those lovely blue and green lines? They all come out black. Therefore, until the day comes when everyone has a colour photocopier, differentiate by weight, not by colour. Figure 8.3 is another example of a line chart.

Bar Charts

Look at the bar chart in Figure 8.4, again from the Toronto Police Service Environmental Scan.

In which year was there the lowest number of reported child abuse offences in Toronto? What was the exact number in 2005?

Chances are you could answer the first question easily, but the third would give you some difficulty. Bar charts give a quick visual impression, but they are vague on the small details. Sometimes a value will be added at the top of each bar so that exact figures can be given. Whether you do this depends on your needs.

Figure 8.3

CRIMINAL CODE INFRACTIONS

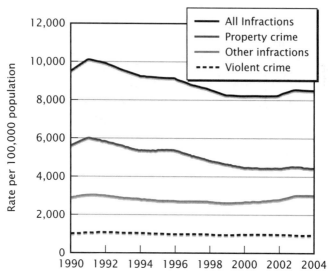

Source: Statistics Canada, "Criminal Code infractions," adapted from the Statistics Canada CANSIM database, Table 252-0013, http://cansim2.statcan.ca.

Figure 8.4

REPORTED CHILD ABUSE OFFENCES

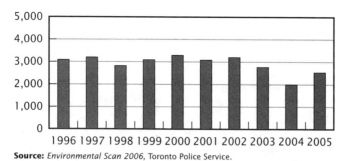

Source: *Environmental Scan 2006,* Toronto Police Service.

Figure 8.4 was a vertical bar chart. Figure 8.5 is an example of a horizontal bar chart.

Figure 8.5

POPULATION WITH DISABILITIES, BY PROVINCE, 2001

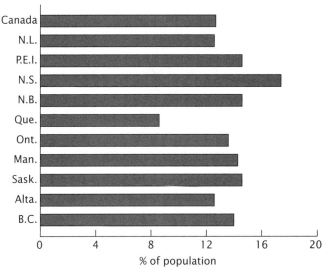

% of population

Source: Adapted from Statistics Canada, "Population with disabilities, by province, 2001," *A Profile of Disability in Canada,* 2001, catalogue 89-577, released December 3, 2003.

Pie Charts

Pie charts are another type of graphic with which you are probably familiar. They make a quick visual impression. Consider Figure 8.6.

Which was the most common decision in adult criminal court in 2003?

Look at Figure 8.7, again from the Toronto Police Service Environmental Scan. Which group made up the largest percentage of uniform police officers in Toronto?

Pie charts can even be used to compare data. Look at Figure 8.8.

In 2003, to which grouping (Canada, province, or local community) did Canadians feel the strongest sense of

Figure 8.6

CRIMINAL CODE CASES IN ADULT CRIMINAL COURT, BY TYPE OF DECISION, 2003

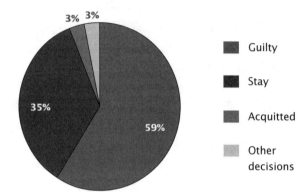

Source: Adapted from Statistics Canada, "Criminal Code cases in adult criminal court, by type of decision, 2003," *JURISTAT—Adult Criminal Court Statistics,* catalogue 85-002, 23(10), page 5, http://www.statcan.ca/bsolc/english/bsolc? catno-85-002-X and also available from Statistics Canada CANSIM database http://cansim2.statcan.ca, Table 252-0045.

Figure 8.7

UNIFORM COMPOSITION, 2005

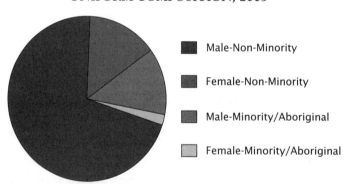

Source: *Environmental Scan 2006,* Toronto Police Service.

Figure 8.8

HOW CANADIANS DESCRIBE THEIR SENSE OF BELONGING TO CANADA, THEIR PROVINCE, AND THEIR COMMUNITY, 2003

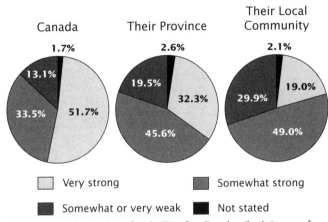

Very strong   Somewhat strong

Somewhat or very weak   Not stated

Source: Adapted from Statistics Canada, "How Canadians describe their sense of belonging to Canada, their province and their community, 2003," *2003 General Social Survey on Social Engagement, Cycle 17: An Overview of Findings*, catalogue 89-598, released July 6, 2004, http://www.statcan.ca/bsolc/english/bsolc?catno= 89-598-X.

belonging? To which did they feel the weakest sense of belonging?

When creating pie charts, keep the following guidelines in mind:

- Make the slices of your pie visually accurate. If you are drawing the graphic manually, rather than on a computer, use a compass and protractor.
- Don't make the slices too tiny. If you have several small categories, group them together under "other" or "miscellaneous."
- Be sure your values add up to your basic whole unit, such as 100 percent or $1.

Where to Place Graphics

Graphics should be placed wherever they'll be most useful. They should not distract readers or disrupt the reading flow. If a graphic is too large to be non-disruptive, place it in an appendix at the back of your report.

Wherever you place the graphic, be sure to refer to it in your text and point out to readers what they should notice in the graphic.

EXPLORATIONS

8.1 In the library, locate a book of government statistics, or go to the Statistics Canada website or a police service website that includes statistical reports or environmental scans. Find a table, line chart, bar chart, and pie chart.

8.2 View the document available at www.torontopolice.on.ca/publications/files/reports/2006envscan.pdf. How are graphics and text used together to help the reader grasp the information given?

8.3 Choose any graphic in this chapter and discuss what you could learn from that graphic. What information could be gleaned from an analysis of the figure or table? What does the graphic tell you?

Chapter 9

The Business Case: Competing for Limited Resources

As in many organizations, police services have limited resources with which to accomplish increasingly complex tasks. Different areas of the service compete for those limited resources. In order to ensure that resources are allocated fairly and effectively, most services require some version of a business case to be presented when resources beyond the normal budget allocation are requested. For example, a business case is completed for purchase of new equipment, for an increase in staffing, even for a change in procedure if the change will have resource implications.

While a business case would not generally be written early in an officer's career, once an officer moves up beyond entry level, business cases await. Their use stems from a policing organization's need to spend every penny wisely (and to be seen to do so). They are called business cases for a reason, since the idea has been taken from the private sector. In businesses, expenditures and operational changes are backed up by cost–benefit analyses—What's the cost? What's the benefit? What else have you considered? Those three questions are at the heart of a business case. Thought about in another way, a business case is the documentation that shows the writer has conducted a careful, detailed investigation of a situation and has reasonable grounds for the recommendations presented. The reader of a business case can weigh the evidence presented and, the writer hopes, agree with those recommendations.

We will be looking at a simplified business case. Business cases often go to the heart of practices and procedures in an organization, and are based on the nitty-gritty specific details of a unit's functioning. Because a real-life business case therefore might not be totally clear to someone outside the organization, we will use as an example a business case based on a fictionalized product, since that requires no insider knowledge on the part of the reader. First, though, look at the following simplified template for a business case:

```
1. Business Case General Information
   Project Name:
   Business Case Author:
   Date:
2. Background
3. Project Impacts
   1. Project Cost
   2. Project Benefits
4. Alternative Solutions Considered
5. Recommendations
```

Let's look at each section briefly before looking at our business case example.

Business Case General Information

This section gives a descriptive title to the business case to let the reader know what the case will be about. It also lists the author and the date the business case was submitted. This section can also include a projected implementation date for the project if the business case is approved.

Background

This section gives the context for the business case, telling the reader what she or he needs to know in order to understand and evaluate the business case. It includes a detailed discussion of the project or resources requested, as well as the need for such a project or resources.

Project Impacts

This section discusses the costs connected with the project, as well as the benefits that would arise from approving the business case. Costs and benefits can be both tangible (money spent or saved, productivity gained) and intangible (increased morale, more credibility, better public relations, and so on). In many organizations, business cases include how the project fits into the organization's service priorities for the year. In the interests of simplicity, we will not do that here.

Alternative Solutions Considered

A business case always includes a section where the writer discusses the alternatives he or she considered before deciding on the recommendation given in the business case. This section has two functions: one, to ensure the writer really has done a thorough analysis of the situation giving rise to the business case and has impartially weighed all options; and two, to demonstrate to the reader that this has been done. One option that is always included is the status quo: what happens if we do nothing at all and keep things as they are? It is important to include this in a business case because most people's natural tendency is to stick with the status quo and not make changes. A writer therefore has to address directly what would or could happen if no change whatsoever is made.

Recommendations

Based on the analysis she or he has done, the writer recommends a course of action. It should flow naturally from the rest of the business case. By this point, the reader should see the necessity and sense of following the writer's recommendation.

Note: Business cases generally include an executive summary. Written last, although placed at the front, the executive summary provides an overview of the entire business case. It summarizes each section of the business case very briefly. An executive summary is usually no longer than one or two paragraphs, but captures the essential points of the entire business case. We are not including an executive summary in the text, but do have an alternate template on the website (www.toserveandprotect.nelson.com) that includes the executive summary, along with a version of the business case sample with this section included.

Let's look at a sample business case, written for a fictional product by a practising police officer. While tongue-in-cheek, it is a well-written example of a persuasive business case (and the writer could make a fortune were he to invent such a product).

Business Case General Information

Project Name: Sticky Nets for Frontline Officers—Less Lethal Force (Technology Acquisition)

Business Case Author: Sgt. Arthur Scott

Background

Big City Police Service (TPS) officers have been involved in situations where lethal force must be used by officers an average of six times per year. Furthermore, an average of three subjects will be shot and killed annually by Big City Police Officers. In BCPS Procedure 15-01—Use of Force, the Big City Police Service has stated that it "places the highest value on the protection of life and the safety of its members and the public, with a greater regard for human life than the protection of property. Members of the Service have a responsibility to only use that force which is reasonably necessary to bring an incident under control effectively and safely." Keeping in mind current budget restraints, this philosophy statement justifies the continuous search for and acquisition of new technologies that increase the safety and decrease the loss of life of both police officers engaged in use of force, and the subjects that they face.

Consistent with this philosophy, Training and Education has identified a new less lethal force technology that will improve the safety of officers while decreasing the loss of life and injury to the public with a cost that is much less than the Taser program request that was denied by the Police Services Board.

The gas operated Sticky Net is a new technology that is considered a less lethal force option for the capture and control of dangerous offenders with minimal risk of injury to subject and officer. Sticky nets (see manufacturer's information in Appendix 1) are an inexpensive, single-use device, about the size of a small fire extinguisher, with a weight of 1.2 kilograms, that is easily deployed from a leg holster. This device, through a compressed carbon dioxide delivery system, deploys a net coated in a poly-mylar (sticky) substance that incorporates trademarked "contracting strand technology" that wraps around and traps the offender. The analogy used by the manufacturer compares this deployment to a spider web trapping and wrapping an insect. The delivery tubes are reusable with replacement Sticky Net and CO_2 cartridges. The device has an effective range up to approx. 90 m (30 feet). This considered a relatively safe distance for officers dealing with subjects not in possession of firearms and demonstrating behaviours that would be, according to the Ontario Use of Force Model, "assaultive" or "lethal force." While this device is not recommended for use against subjects armed with firearms, this may be an option within a tactical deployment.

Sticky nets have been proven safe in laboratory testing by both the manufacturer and in independent testing by the U.S. Department of Justice (see Appendix 2: "Testing"). The device has also been used extensively by several large American policing agencies that have given it very favorable reviews and high rates of success (see Appendix 3: "Testimonials"). Recently the device was approved for use in Ontario by the Ministry of Community Safety and Security, although there are no other police agencies in Ontario yet using it.

Recently the Service considered the use of the Taser for frontline officers, but the request was denied by the Police Service Board due to cost factors. The Sticky Net is considered a reasonable alternative to that device at a fraction of the cost.

This proposal recommends that the Service provide training on Sticky Net technology to all frontline officers over the next three years. That will annualize to 3,600 officers trained over three years starting in January 2008. It is also recommended that the Service purchase sufficient supplies of Sticky nets to replace equipment used by officers. It is anticipated that the use of Sticky nets by frontline officers will reduce injuries to officers, reduce injuries to members of the public, and reduce the liability of the Service in instances of use of force.

Project Impacts

The annual operational funding for this project will be as follows:

2008	1200 units issued	$180,000.00
	Divisional Stock	127,500.00
2009	1200 units issued	180,000.00
	Divisional Stock	127,500.00
2010	1200 units issued	180,000.00
	Divisional Stock	127,500.00
Total project cost		$922,500.00

Annual maintenance after 2010: $200,000.00 (based on current pricing)

This can be compared to the 10 million dollars that would be required to equip 3,600 officers with Tasers. Substantial costs in the Taser program are also realized with replacement batteries and cartridges totalling up to 2 million dollars annually, depending on use.

The sole supplier of Sticky Net technology is New Mid West Policing Supplies. There is no comparable product. The current unit price is as follows:

Complete Unit	$150.00 (bulk order 2,000 units)—with reusable cylinder
Sticky Net Cartridge	$100.00 (bulk order 2,000 units)—single use
CO_2 Cartridges	$25.00 (bulk order 2,000 units)—single use

New Mid West has guaranteed a three-week turnaround on orders.

Training will be delivered as a half-day course during officers' annual Use of Force Training. Use of Force Trainers will attend a two-day qualification course provided by the manufacturer at no cost to the Service, based on a three-year contract.

Nominal cost is involved in cleanup and release of subject from the Sticky Net. Cleanup involves the use of a 2.5% acetic acid solution (vinegar available from any grocery store, with 50% water). The vinegar—water solution immediately neutralizes the poly-mylar sticky substance and dissolves the contracting strands. The solution is easily delivered from a spray bottle. A $3 container of vinegar will clean up approximately ten applications.

Sticky Net technology will enhance officer safety and reduce injuries to officers in the line of duty. This will have a long-term positive financial impact on the organization.

Sticky Net technology will also reduce injury and death to members of the public, which will reduce officer and Service exposure to SIU investigations, civil litigation, and defence of criminal allegations. This will have long-term positive impacts on the Service financially, and on individual members' morale and wellness.

Alternative Solutions Considered

As previously identified in this Business Case, the preferred technology for the frontline officer is the Taser. However, the Police Service Board has only been willing to approve the use of the Taser for frontline supervisors. It is not the intent of this Business Case to disrupt the current use of the Taser by frontline supervisors, but to provide a viable, cost-effective, less-lethal alternative technology to frontline officers. An alternative would be for the Board to approve the Business Case previously submitted for the supply of the Taser to frontline officers. The financial impact of the Taser is about $10 million more over three years than this Sticky Net technology proposal. The Taser will also have a much higher annual cost (as previously noted above) to maintain the program.

Another alternative is to not supply frontline officers with additional less-lethal technology. This choice would have numerous negative impacts on the Service. First, numerous inquests have recommended that the Service should explore less-lethal force options as the technology arises. Continuing to equip officers with the latest less-lethal options demonstrates good faith on the part of the Service to minimize the use of lethal force by officers. Second, potentially preventable injuries and death will occur to officers and the public. Finally, Sticky Nets are a tool to reduce Service risk exposure in low-frequency, high-risk use-of-force events. The Service must show due diligence in the protection of life and prevention of injury to officers and members of the public.

Recommendations

1. To implement the purchasing, training, and equipping of frontline officers with the Sticky Net technology in January 2008.

2. To proceed with this program in January 2008, according to the Service Management Cycle Guidelines, funding must be committed by September 1, 2007.

Source: Courtesy of Scott Weidmark.

EXPLORATIONS

And now it's your turn. Utilize the Business Case template given above to complete one of the business cases in the following Explorations. The business case topics suggested in the Explorations are based on real programs or initiatives that you can research. You will then write the business case as though you were proposing the initiative for your service, which does not yet have such a program.

The topics all require some research, and some critical and creative thinking on your part. You will likely not be able to find precise details about the cost of the projects; instead, be as realistic as possible. Be sure to detail alternatives in your business case, including staying with the status quo. Make a clear recommendation that your project be approved.

To simplify the assignment, each of the following Explorations includes some websites to visit to get you started on the project. Additional business case topics can be found on the companion website.

An evaluation sheet for the business case follows the Explorations.

9.1 Many police departments utilize a Domestic Violence Emergency Response System (DVERS). Research DVERS, and write a business case for such a system based on the programs you find. Here are some websites to get you started:

www.victimservicestoronto.com/dv_emergency_ response.htm

www.dixonhouse.ca/dvers.html

www.innovation-award.ca/story8f56.html?Page=story .html&IdeabookID=522

www.cal-dufvictimservices.ca/dvers

http://search.hipinfo.info/details.asp?RSN=14224

www.adt.ca/en/about/communityinvolvement/dvers.asp

9.2 Police officers have a higher rate of suicide, alcohol abuse, and marriage breakdown than almost any other profession. Check out the following website to gain information on a unique program in which former police officers counsel current officers who are attempting to cope with job stress:

http://ubhc.umdnj.edu/cop2cop/main.htm. Write a business case for a similar program in your community. Here are some websites to get you started:

http://ubhc.umdnj.edu/cop2cop/main.htm

http://njintouch.state.nj.us/personnel/newsroom/press_07/07-08-01.htm

www.cophealth.com/articles/peersupp.html

9.3 Police Services across Canada have partnered with the RCMP and the Alzheimer Society to set up a voluntary Wandering Persons Registry for people with dementia. Research the Registry, and, pretending it does not yet exist, write a business case for establishing the Registry in your community.

www.alzheimer.ca/english/safelyhome/benefits.htm

www.alzheimer.ca/english/safelyhome/managing.htm

www.fredericton.ca/en/publicsafety/resources/Police-Wandering-Persons-Registry-Form.pdf

www.alzheimerhuron.on.ca/wandering.shtml

Table 9.1

BUSINESS CASE EVALUATION

	Fail (Below 60%)	Minimum Pass (60–69%)	Solid Pass (70–79%)	Pass with Excellence (80–100%)
Business Case General Information				
Background				
Project Impacts: • Costs • Benefits				
Alternative Solutions Considered				
Recommendations				

Chapter 10

Writing in a Postsecondary Setting

Traditionally, the basic educational requirement to join a police service has been a Grade 12 diploma. For example, the Ontario Police Services Act gives the following admission requirements for constables:

Ontario Police Services Act, Section 43(1)

43. (1) No person shall be appointed as a police officer unless he or she,
    (a) is a Canadian citizen or a permanent resident of Canada;
    (b) is at least eighteen years of age;
    (c) is physically and mentally able to perform the duties of the position, having regard to his or her own safety and the safety of members of the public;
    (d) is of good moral character and habits; and
    (e) has successfully completed at least four years of secondary school education or its equivalent.

Source: Police Services Act, Revised Statutes of Ontario 1990. Copyright © Queen's Printer for Ontario.

The current reality, however, is quite different.

At a convocation ceremony on June 17, 2008, at which he received an honorary degree from Humber College, Toronto Police Chief Bill Blair contrasted the typical situation thirty-two years ago when he joined the force, "when it was unusual for any police officer recruit to possess any post-secondary education" to the current situation when "68 percent of everyone we [Toronto Police Service] hire today brings with them a post secondary degree or diploma." As well, practising police officers are pursuing postsecondary education in record numbers. In the past, a few officers earned degrees by spending years—often up to a decade and a half—taking night school courses semester after semester. (Chief Blair earned his bachelor's degree at the University of Toronto in this manner.) Innovative programs such as the Leadership Enhancement diploma at Humber College and the BAA in Justice Studies at the University of Guelph-Humber have met the pent-up desire of officers to continue their education, and have met the needs of their organizations as well. In the same address Chief Blair spoke of Toronto police officers studying in these programs who "come back and challenge my organization, and challenge me with what they have learned. We are a strong organization as a result."

In earlier chapters we have discussed the various roles and characteristics of writing in a police setting. What are the roles of writing in an academic setting?

Roles of Academic Writing

While writing in a postsecondary institution can be summarized as that of arguing a thesis, the roles of writing can be broken down further.

Writing As Thinking on Paper

First, writing can be seen as thinking on paper, as a writer struggling to articulate an idea so that she or he can grasp its implications. This role has been expressed by E. M. Forster: "How can I know what I think until I see what I say?" Writing in a postsecondary institution, especially in the drafting stage, is used to clarify thinking. An unexpressed idea hardly lives at all.

Writing As Dialogue

Writing in an academic setting is also a dialogue. A postsecondary institution is a community of scholars. Different members of that community are at different stages of their scholarly journey. Undergraduates, especially at the beginning of their program, are rookies, while professors and the authors of the material read and discussed are seasoned veterans. Any professional, though, will tell you that the insights of a rookie can be invaluable. And academic debate is honestly valued in a postsecondary institution. Knowledge is increased by questioning, challenging, and taking thoughts further.

Writing As Taking a Stand

Knowledge is increased by taking a stand. I said that one could summarize the role of academic writing as that of arguing a thesis. A thesis is a point the writer wishes to prove in his essay. Arguing a thesis always means taking a stand. Academic writing values a writer's researching, thinking about, struggling with, and then taking a stand on an issue.

Writing As Exercising the Brain

At the same time, writing in a postsecondary setting is sometimes intellectual weightlifting. To train cognitive muscles, as it were, students are sometimes asked to play the devil's advocate (literally, defence lawyer for the devil) and argue the other side of an issue. In an academic setting, it is important to see all sides of an issue, to develop a broad perspective, and to suspend judgment until a full examination of an issue has been undertaken.

Effective Academic Writing

We have spoken about the characteristics of police writing that are valued. What characteristics are valued in academic writing? A strong focus and an organized structure are essential, along with a clear, sourced argument; that is, a logical presentation of a well-supported thesis developed through research that is documented in the essay. Postsecondary writing is not simply a regurgitation of the research a writer has done; rather, what is valued is the quality of thought that the student demonstrates and what the student has done to incorporate and integrate the research of others into his or her own stance on an issue or topic.

This may sound like a tall order, but research on effective writing shows that writing well is a learned skill. Students are not born able to write essays. Like any skill, its mastery comes more easily to some than to others, but anyone can learn to be an effective writer. Again, like any skill, writing must be practised, but practised mindfully. Just like the golfer who keeps practising the same bad swing and gets no better, a writer who doesn't analyze his or her strengths, specific weaknesses, and areas that need improvement, and therefore doesn't put what has been learned into practice, is not going to improve.

Effective writers appear to know this, and utilize strategies and processes to improve their writing; research indicates that ineffective writers tend to think that good writers are born and that it's hopeless, so why bother. If you have ever felt like that, read on. Here's what effective writers know:

- The toughest part of writing for anyone is getting started.
- The most important work in writing is often done before beginning.

"Writing is easy: All you do is sit staring at a blank sheet of paper until drops of blood form on your forehead." (Gene Fowler)

"Every writer I know has trouble writing." (Joseph Heller)

The Writing Process: Prewriting

"You can't wait for inspiration. You have to go after it with a club." (Jack London)

Effective writers find a strategy to get themselves going. They try different prewriting techniques, learn about themselves as writers, and use that learning to improve.

There are a variety of prewriting techniques. Interestingly, different techniques work for different people. For instance, I find brainstorming and mental rehearsing effective; I'm not a visual person, so I don't use clustering or mind mapping. I couldn't freewrite to save my life. Others swear by these techniques. The point is, an effective writer figures out what techniques work for him or her and then utilizes those techniques to overcome that major obstacle—the blank page.

Here are some techniques, along with examples.

Mental Rehearsing

Mental rehearsing is talking through a piece of writing with yourself before putting pen to paper or fingers to keyboard. Some people who appear to compose quite easily and quickly have actually spent a great deal of time working out the piece in their heads, thinking of strategies and approaches. As they drive, as they walk, even as they sleep, they chew on the writing problem. They may still use another prewriting technique when they actually begin to write, but much of the work has already been done internally before moving to an external manifestation. I can't display an example of this prewriting technique, but the next time you see someone sit down and write seemingly with ease, ask how long he or she had been thinking about the piece before beginning.

> "The best time for planning a book is while you're doing the dishes." (Agatha Christie)

Brainstorming

Brainstorming is generating ideas about a topic and writing them down without prematurely rejecting any given idea. It's a deliberately messy process to allow ideas to flow. The example on the next two pages is a scanned version of the original very

Figure 10.1

BRAINSTORMING

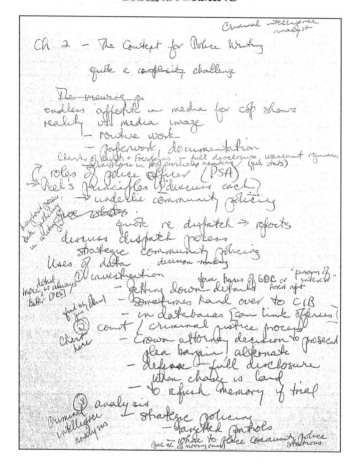

rough brainstorming I did for Chapter 2 of this text. What differences do you see between the original brainstorming and the finished chapter? (Note: My brainstorming is fairly linear, a semi-outline, because I also use mental rehearsing. Brainstorming is not always this targeted. Rather, it can be ideas tumbling from the brain to the page in a seemingly chaotic way. If that's how you brainstorm, go with it.)

Figure 10.1 (continued)

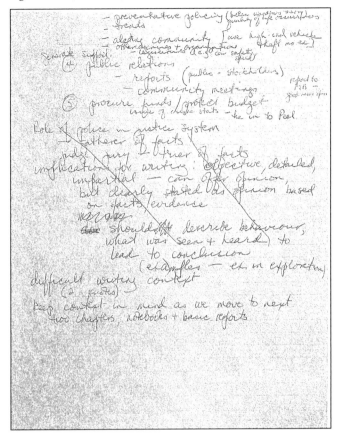

Clustering or Mind Mapping

Clustering works well for visual learners. Generally, the writer begins with the topic in a circle in the centre of the page. He or she then generates ideas that flow from that topic. Each idea can be a spark for another thought. This technique is sometimes called webbing, because the result can resemble a spider's web, with ideas intersecting with one another. Here's an example of how a visual learner (not me!) might have approached Chapter 2.

Figure 10.2

MIND MAPPING

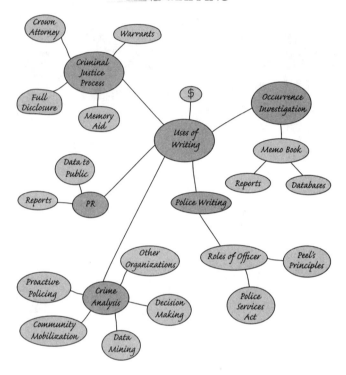

W5-H

W5-H is the classic journalism strategy: who, what, where, when, why, how. A writer asks these questions about his or her topic, and uses the resulting answers as a starting point. Figure 10.3 is an example based on the discussion of the incident and/or General Occurrence Report in Chapter 4 (page 76).

Outlining

Outlining is likely the prewriting technique that is most familiar to people, since generations of school children have been taught how to outline. An outline is a useful tool, but a

Figure 10.3

W5-H

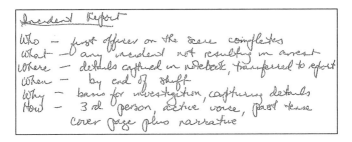

Incident Report

Who — first officer on the scene completes
What — any incident not resulting in arrest
Where — details captured in notebook, transferred to report
When — by end of shift
Why — basis for investigation, capturing details
How — 3rd person, active voice, past tense
Cover page plus narrative

writer must be careful not to become straightjacketed by writing an outline too soon in the writing process. An outline is probably a good second or third prewriting step. Figure 10.4 is an outline for Chapter 2.

Freewriting

Freewriting is a technique that works well for some people, especially when they are confronted by writer's block. The most difficult part of writing is getting started at all. I remember that when I was writing my doctoral dissertation I had the cleanest floors in town because every time I didn't want to write a new chapter, I'd wash my floors. What's your writing avoidance behaviour? Whatever it is, freewriting is designed to overcome that resistance. With freewriting a writer sets a time limit—say, five minutes—and writes without stopping for that time period. It doesn't matter what he or she writes; the point is to write without stopping, almost like a stream of consciousness. Only at the end of the time limit does the writer stop and look back at what was written and decide if something is usable. I'm not much of a freewriter, but please see my sample in Figure 10.5.

As stated, not all techniques work for all people. Give them a try, and keep the ones that work for you.

Figure 10.4

OUTLINING

Outline – Chapter Two

I. Bkgd. – increase in writing
  – examples
II. Roles of police officer
  A. Peel's Principles
  B. PSA
III. Uses of police writing
  A. Occurrence investigation
    – notebook
    – reports
    – databases
  B. Criminal justice process
    – warrants
    – Crown Attorney
    – full disclosure
    – laid to memory before trial
  C. Incident/crime analysis
    – allocation of resources / $ #
      decision making
    – data-mining – quality of
      life issues
    – community policing
    – use by other organizations
      – examples
  D. Public relations
    – garner public support
      – community meetings
    – reports
  E. Financial support
    – value for dollar

The Writing Process: Drafting

Once they're done with the prewriting stage, effective writers move on to drafting. And there's something else effective writers tend to know that ineffective writers don't.

"The first draft of anything is shit." (Ernest Hemingway)

Figure 10.5

FREEWRITING

Example of freewriting

Why is it that freewriting works for some people? Writing researchers seem to find/think that it does, but it never has for me! I find freewriting really aggravating—my mind just doesn't work that way—too left brain or something; I hate to write without some sort of plan. Of course, I don't mind changing plans or getting rid of stuff, so maybe that's it. Maybe some people need freewriting or benefit from it because it allows them to dump ideas on the page without worrying about them. I want to stop and consider/reflect on this now rather than keep writing. That is really annoying that I'm supposed to just keep going. I guess I don't worry too much about the correctness of what I'm writing until I revise, so I don't tend to want to freewrite because my brainstorming gives me enough freedom to get started. I'm stopping now because my arm/elbow hurts from writing like this. Bleah!

[Note: please don't let the above rant stop you from trying freewriting — it really does/works (very well) for some people!]

Hemingway may have stated this a bit crudely, but his words point to a crucial bit of knowledge: It ain't over till it's over. A rough draft is only a beginning. It lets you see what you have before you kick it up a notch. There is real freedom in that knowledge. A writer can take risks in a rough draft, try things that might be eliminated into the final version of the essay but, on the other hand, that might lead to an original, creative insight. (Painters call this a "happy accident.")

In a rough draft, things don't need to be perfect. Grammar and spelling can be corrected in the proofreading stage, and some missing pieces added later. For example, as I wrote the rough draft of various chapters of this text, I utilized a code of square brackets and full caps [LIKE THIS] to indicate any place I needed to add something. I used this when I didn't have the exact reference I needed, or if the right word wasn't presenting itself, or when a section was proving difficult to write at that point. I could then go back and revise relatively easily afterward, and that little roadblock didn't stop me in the drafting stage. A first draft is getting the thoughts on paper, full speed ahead.

The Writing Process: Revision

"Half my life is an act of revision." (John Irving)

"I'm not a very good writer, but I'm an excellent rewriter." (James Michener)

The revision portion of the writing process is where effective writers shine and ineffective writers sputter. Ineffective writers tend to barely proofread; they're so anxious to be finished with this loathsome task that it's like the old children's game of hot potato—they can't wait to hand an essay in as soon as the draft is done.

Adequate writers proofread for grammar and mechanics. Good writers actually revise. "Revision" means "to see again"—to look at the draft with new eyes. Good writers go through a draft many times, looking at it through several lenses. They look at content, clarity of thought, logical structure. They consider whether portions of the essay should be moved, or expressed differently. Are transitions needed? Is it clear how one idea leads to the next, how adjacent thoughts are connected? Effective writers also revise with their ears.

They read the essay out loud or to themselves, paying attention to the sound of their sentences. And they also proofread for grammar and mechanics.

They do this mindfully as well. People are creatures of habit, and have habitual errors. For example, I don't make an infinite number of errors, but I do tend to re-make the same errors. Even when typing, my fingers are going to mess up in a predictable way. And so I'm especially careful when proofreading to look for these habitual mistakes.

The Bottom Line

In summary, here is what postsecondary teachers expect in an essay:

- A clear thesis: an explicitly stated arguable point
- An organized, logical structure
- An argument that is supported by more than your opinion
- APA documentation

The following are student essays. The first two ("Exposing the Innocent" and "Sarasota County Sheriff's Office: Being Accountable to the Community") deal with the Sarasota Sheriff's Office Arrest Card website mentioned in Chapter 4, Exploration 4.1. Note how each essay writer takes a stand and argues a thesis in regard to that website.

Exposing the Innocent

Many societies struggle with the delicate balancing act of exposing those accused of crimes and protecting their privacy. In Sarasota, Florida, the practice of releasing information on arrested individuals is endorsed and readily available. This essay will prove that by providing intimate details of arrests on the Internet, the Sarasota County Sheriff's Office is subjecting those accused of committing crimes to a number of unfair risks and biases.

As a state, Florida has been known for having a strict and unforgiving justice system. Within mere hours or days of arrest, accused persons who are supposedly presumed innocent are paraded on the official Internet website of the Sarasota County Sheriff's Office. The website displays colour photographs of the arrested parties along with their birth dates, arrest dates, charges, addresses, and employment details. This information is available on a user-friendly website that is updated on a regular basis.

With the widespread use of computers and free access made available in many public facilities, virtually anyone in the world can obtain the details on people arrested in Sarasota in a matter of seconds. As such, the arrested parties are subjected to a number of risks. One of the gravest concerns is that of vigilantism. A victim of crime or one of their supporters could be tempted to seek revenge on an accused. In cases that are particularly heinous, complete strangers could be motivated to confront one of these individuals. By revealing residential addresses, the Sheriff's Office is informing vigilantes of the exact locations to find those accused of offences and commit further crimes against them.

The accused parties are also at risk of losing their social connections. By having their employment status and details revealed to prospective employers, these individuals and their companies could be losing business opportunities. Most of the people posted on the website are listed as unemployed, and the publicity they receive in this forum will only aggravate their current circumstances. The parties may also find that their neighbours and friends treat them differently after seeing their profiles online. At a time when they need strong social connections more than ever, those placed before the criminal justice system are actually being put at risk for further isolation by the actions of the Sheriff's Office.

The financial security of the accused parties is also placed in danger due to the website. By showing photographs and providing personal details such as birth dates and addresses, the website is exposing information that should be kept tightly guarded. An unethical person could take these details from the website and use them for an assortment of fraudulent purposes. Whether using the information to apply for a credit card or impersonate the accused in some other fashion, the increased risk of the information being used for a sinister purpose is unfair.

Another concern for the accused parties is the possibility that they will not receive fair trials due to the Internet exposure. Witnesses have the opportunity to view this public website and study the faces of the accused persons they may have to identify in court proceedings sometime in the future. This may provide an unfair advantage as they will not have to recall the images of the perpetrators from memory work alone. Potential jurors could also view the website and have images of booking photographs in their minds when deciding guilt or innocence.

The Sarasota County Sheriff's Office places accused persons in compromising positions in a number of ways. Their safety, social opportunities, and security are all compromised by what is being displayed on a website available worldwide. The information is so detailed and readily available that many people could be tempted to misuse it. In creating and endorsing this website, the Sarasota County Sheriff's Office is exposing accused persons to unfair risks before they have even been tried in a courtroom or convicted of a crime.

REFERENCES

Sarasota County Sheriff's Office. (2008). *Daily arrest cards.* Retrieved April 18, 2008, from http://sarasotasheriff.org/arrests.asp

Source: Courtesy of Sergeant Jennifer Johnson.

Sarasota County Sheriff's Office: Being Accountable to the Community

The Sarasota County Sheriff's Office publishes daily arrest reports pertaining to persons arrested on the previous date or, in the case of weekends or holidays, persons arrested since the last business day. Some may argue that releasing this information to the public in such a free-flowing manner breaches a person's rights or puts their safety or the safety of the law enforcement officers who arrest them in jeopardy. The aim of this essay is to respectfully argue that the Sarasota County Sheriff's Office is acting responsibly and following up on the positive work of their officers with an effective proactive approach that serves as a deterrent.

The arrest cards include a photograph of the suspect, along with their name, date of birth, address, location of arrest, and the charge(s). This may seem like an infringement of a person's rights as one is presumed innocent until proven guilty; however, the same information becomes part of the public record anyway once the matter is brought before the courts. There is no doubt that this method of disseminating the information makes it accessible to the public in an easier and more expedient manner, but this is merely the product of the modern-day Internet. In publishing daily arrest reports, the Sarasota County Sheriff's Office is not releasing any information that would not be released eventually, and is therefore not breaching a person's rights.

The website does not jeopardize the safety of suspects or arresting officers. As mentioned, the personal information contained in the daily arrest reports eventually becomes part of the public record. One may argue that, generally speaking, some of the less serious crimes listed in the reports would not normally receive media or public attention and suspects' photographs would not be shown to the community. However, any citizen has the right to attend court and observe proceedings, therefore having the opportunity to view a suspect in person. If one was determined to seek revenge or participate in any sort of vigilantism it would not make a difference whether they viewed a suspect's photograph on the website or attended court and viewed them in person. As for the safety of the arresting officers, most law-enforcement agencies already require officers to have their name on their uniforms, making them readily identifiable. An officer's name published on the website in most cases should not be cause for any added concern.

Daily arrest reports allow the Sarasota County Sheriff's Office to effectively showcase the talents of individual officers and relate back to the community the excellent effort the organization is putting forth with the goal of public safety in mind. It not only allows the community to see the positive aspects of the work being done, but also allows them to monitor arrest rates and trends, thereby allowing them to have some degree of accountability over the police.

The website holds the criminal element or those considering breaking the law accountable and acts as a deterrent. It may not matter much to a seasoned criminal whether or not his or her identity is known in the community, but it would likely make those who are on the borderline think twice before participating in criminal activity. One example may be a normally law-abiding citizen who consumes too much alcohol and is contemplating driving a motor vehicle. The fear of being on the daily arrest report in some cases would cause them to reconsider their actions and cause others to intervene on their behalf.

In closing, the examples and arguments listed in this essay respectfully support the Sarasota County Sheriff's Office in relation to the release of daily arrest reports. The practice is a responsible way of reporting public information back to the community and holds both police and citizens accountable.

REFERENCES

Sarasota County Sheriff's Office. (2008). *Daily arrest card*. Retrieved April 17, 2008, from http://sarasotasheriff.org/arrests.asp

Source: Courtesy of Staff Sergeant John Whitworth.

The next two student essays ("The CSI Myth: Fingerprint Methods on Television and the Problems Caused in Court" and "Downtown Toronto Congestion: Cause and Cure") demonstrate two methods of essay development, the first through comparison and the second through causal analysis.

The CSI Myth: Fingerprint Methods on Television and the Problems Caused in Court

Television has taken great liberties in its portrayal of police officers but for the most part I'm sure the public saw the difference between these programs and reality. The forensic sciences, however, have always been clouded in mystery. No one really knew what a forensic investigator did, until *CSI* was created, that is. *CSI* has both educated society and at the same time misled it, causing a myriad of problems in the courtroom. As a forensic investigator with the Toronto Police Service, I have experienced firsthand how the disparity between real life and television has influenced the criminal justice system and the need to reverse this trend.

On *CSI* the process of collecting and identifying of fingerprints is significantly embellished. In one particular episode, the CSI officer attended a gruesome murder scene and proceeded directly to the bathroom where the body was found. She began to examine the white porcelain tub using a feather duster, luminescent powders, and an ultraviolet light. As the powder floated through the air, the lighting effects were particularly dazzling. The examiner managed to locate one small piece of a fingerprint that was taken to the lab and loaded into a computer. As everyone waited anxiously, the computer miraculously produced an exact match, complete with a photograph of the suspect. After a short commercial break, the suspect was brought to another part of the lab where he was questioned and the case was closed.

Unfortunately, very little of what is seen on *CSI* is possible at a real crime scene. When the call comes in for a homicide, it takes me the first sixty minutes just to prepare my equipment and crew. Once at the location, but before entering, I don a white protective suit that covers almost every inch of my skin. Hours of photography and videotape are completed before anything is touched, and fingerprinting is often the very last examination because of the mess it causes. I would examine a bathtub with a regular brush and either black or dark grey powder under regular bright white light. This is a very tedious procedure that doesn't cast any dark blue or purple glow around the room. If I am lucky enough to find fingerprints, which is far rarer than on television, I submit them to a computer operator who performs a search of the database. The computer gives approximately fifteen possible suspects, not a match, and the operator has to manually determine if there is a criminal identification. The process of matching fingerprints is both long and boring, following a procedure of analysis, comparison, evaluation, and verification often done by three or more examiners before the suspect information is released. Worst of all, I never get to speak to that suspect, let alone try and break him for a confession. My job was done when I left the scene.

What *CSI* writers do is take one forensic procedure and exaggerate it. The problem arises when juries watch these programs and are left wondering why the forensic investigator didn't find any fingerprints. Eyewitness accounts of suspects in possession of property are being questioned when there are no fingerprints or other forensic evidence found. I have personally faced a jury that looked bewildered as a defence attorney questioned me relentlessly about why no fingerprints were found on bullets. The answer is actually very simple: they almost never are, but the jury has watched television and they know it can be done.

Changes must occur in the judicial system to right the wrong impressions left by television. The Crown Attorney must provide expert witnesses to explain the real procedures of forensic science and reinforce these during opening and closing arguments. The judge has a responsibility to properly charge a jury with regard to forensic science and what it is capable of, and as the forensic investigator, I must be prepared to give detailed testimony and explanations to ensure that a jury understands what can and cannot be done at a crime scene. We have come a long way since *Dragnet* and *Barney Miller*, but the magic performed on *CSI* is still a glimpse of the future.

REFERENCES

Hankin, G. (2001). Essential knowledge for fingerprint analysis and comparison. *Identification Canada*, 24(2), 4—11.

Thomas, A. P. (2006). The CSI effect: Fact or fiction. *The Yale Law Journal Pocket Part 70.* Retrieved September 23, 2007, from http://yalelawjournal.org/2006/02/thomas.html

Source: Courtesy of Paul White.

Downtown Toronto Congestion: Cause and Cure

Traffic in the downtown core of Toronto is gridlocked from sunup till well beyond sundown every day of the week. It would be easy to blame this congestion on the ever-increasing reliance on the automobile, antiquated road infrastructure, and a reluctance to utilize public transit. I would agree that these factors are a part of the problem, but I would suggest, based on my twenty years of policing the downtown core, that there are other factors at play that are equally if not more responsible for the congestion.

The road network in downtown Toronto has remained the same for the last fifty years. Initiatives such as synchronized signals and one-way streets have been instituted in an attempt to increase the efficiency of the overburdened road network. However, there is no room to expand the arterial road network. In fact, a significant portion of the downtown road network was recently demolished with the dismantling of the Gardiner Expressway east of the Don Valley Parkway.

Environmentalists saw the dismantling of this section of the Gardiner as a victory. Many claimed that the area had somehow been beautified and they are right; there is nothing more beautiful than the sight of hundreds of vehicles backed up in traffic as a result. In my opinion, the move to dismantle this portion of the Gardiner was shortsighted. Little if any consideration was given to the displaced traffic, other than it now sits on Lakeshore Boulevard waiting for traffic signal after traffic signal.

Many environmentalists, including Mayor Miller, have suggested that the entire Gardiner expressway should be dismantled. Once again, a shortsighted move, as no consideration has been given to the displaced traffic. There have been suggestions of constructing a tunnel under the Toronto harbour to absorb the traffic; however, I would suggest the costs of this project would be prohibitive. The consequences of this very proposal were demonstrated this past winter when ice buildup on the CN tower caused the closing of the Gardiner for over a week. The ensuing gridlock was unbearable and resulted in numerous complaints to the police.

The Chair of the Toronto Transit Commission (TTC) has suggested that King Street should be designated as a streetcar-only route through the downtown core. Once again, a shortsighted suggestion. The result of such a closure was clearly demonstrated this past May when a significant portion of King Street was closed due to falling granite from First Canadian Place. The resulting gridlock was unbearable and numerous complaints were lodged.

Public transit, for those who live in Toronto, is a viable alternative to using a car. For those that live beyond the borders of the City of Toronto, however, public transit, although available, is not a reasonable alternative. GO transit service serves the corridor from Hamilton to Oshawa quite well, but it does not service the northern communities of the GTA. Although transit is available, the time involved in the commute is unreasonable. For most the automobile is the only practical method for commuting back and forth to Toronto for employment.

The challenge therefore is to ensure the efficiency of the existing road network. Bylaws have been enacted designating all arterial roads as rush hour routes. Vehicles are prohibited from stopping on these routes during the morning and evening rush hours. The intent is to keep the routes clear to allow for the free flow of traffic. Unfortunately, the motoring public does not pay attention to the bylaws and parks whenever and wherever they want. As a result the roads are congested and traffic crawls along at a snail's pace. In many cases motorists end up trapped in intersections, blocking the flow of the opposing traffic and causing complete gridlock at some of the downtown intersections.

There is also a great deal of construction occurring in the downtown core. Many of the old warehouses are being converted into loft condos and many are being demolished to be replaced by high-rise towers. Traditionally the developers were forced to hire paid duty police officers to control access to and from their sites. Permits were issued with the condition that arterial roads be kept clear during the rush hour periods. Recently the City has issued permits to the developers allowing for the permanent closure of a lane of traffic during the construction period. This change certainly favours the developers but has caused a great deal of congestion as a result.

The TTC must maintain numerous kilometres of streetcar tracks. During the time of writing, the summer of 2007, Dundas Street through the downtown core is closed while the Commission replaces the streetcar tracks. Dundas Street is a very busy arterial route as well as a streetcar route. All of the traffic normally found on Dundas Street has been displaced onto the other available routes, causing them to be even more congested.

Toronto is still known as Hollywood North. On any given day there can be several film shoots occurring on the streets of Toronto. Permits for film shoots are issued by the Toronto Film Office without consultation from the Roads Department who is responsible for the coordination of construction projects. On many occasions permits have been issued by both offices for adjoining locations, causing backlogs that last for miles.

Toronto is also home to the world. Toronto has been described as the most diverse city on the planet. On numerous occasions throughout the year, street festivals, parades, and demonstrations are held to celebrate and/or protest the diversity of the communities that make up Toronto. Toronto also hosts Gay Pride, Caribana, and the Santa Claus Parade on the streets of downtown Toronto. Most if not all of these events occur on the streets in the downtown core. Fifty-Two Division, the downtown division, accommodated 842 special events in 2006 and is on pace to break 950 in 2007. All of these permits are issued by the City Special Events Office without consultation with the Film Office or the Roads Department.

There is hope, however, and I will offer a few suggestions to ease the gridlock. First, a comprehensive traffic plan for the downtown area must be prepared. Believe it or not, at the present time one does not exist. The planning team must include the City, the police, and the traffic engineers in order for the plan to be effective.

Once a traffic plan is developed, a joint planning team must be established which includes the City of Toronto, the Roads Department, the Film Office, the Special Events Office, the Police Service, the Fire Service, the TTC, and the Ambulance Service. A coordinated approach to construction, filming, special events, and road closures must be established to ease the congestion in the downtown core. This team must have the authority to refuse permit applications if the event is projected to congest the road network.

Finally, a coordinated enforcement campaign supported by a media campaign is necessary to send home the message that courteous motoring is the best method to ease the gridlock in the downtown core. No stopping means no stopping. It is an offence to block an intersection. These messages must be delivered.

Yes, congestion can be blamed on the increasing reliance on the automobile, an antiquated road network, and a reluctance to utilize public transit. However, as discussed there are other factors at play that are equally responsible for the congestion. If these factors are addressed, the congestion in the downtown core can be significantly reduced.

APA Documentation

"APA" stands for the American Psychological Association, the professional body of scholars in the social science field. Since students and professionals in justice studies are in the social science field, APA documentation conventions are used in essays, research papers, and published work.

Why Do We Document?

There are three basic reasons why we use documentation in papers:

- Give credit where credit is due: while a thesis-driven paper shows the writer's position on a topic, that position is grounded in others' work, which must be acknowledged
- Allow the reader to evaluate our sources for currency and credibility
- Allow the reader to read what we read: this is how knowledge is advanced, by our sharing the signposts to new insights. Documentation entries include elements that will allow readers to find the actual works we read.

How Do We Document?

Here is the *standard format* for an APA entry, followed by an example:

Last name, initial. (Year). *Title*. City: Publisher.
Ashworth, A. (2005). *Sentencing and criminal justice*. (4th ed.) Cambridge: Cambridge University Press.

All other entries are variations on this basic theme. Note that with the exception of journal titles (below), titles of works only have the first word capitalized; the rest of the title is in lowercase. The first word of a subtitle is also capitalized.

Here's a *book with two authors*:

Last name, initials. (Year). *Title*. City: Publisher.

Roberts, J. V., & Hough, M. (2005).*Understanding public atti-
tudes to criminal justice*. Maidenhead: Open University
Press.

The entry for *an article in a collection* focuses on the article,
then the book in which it was published:

Last name of author of article, initial. (Year). Title of article. In
Initial of editor, last name (Ed.), *Title*. City: Publisher.

La Prairie, C. (2007). Aboriginal overrepresentation: No
single problem, no simple solution. In J. V. Roberts &
M. G. Grossman (Eds.), *Criminal justice in Canada: A
reader*. Toronto: Nelson.

Scholarly essays are published in peer-reviewed journals.
A peer-reviewed journal, as opposed to a magazine, is written
not for the general public, but for professionals in a given field.
Articles are submitted to the journal by scholars in the field,
and other experts review the article before recommending
whether or not it should be published. As opposed to most
magazine articles, articles in scholarly journals are expected to
advance the knowledge and thinking in that field, not merely
entertain.

Journals are published several times a year (typically three
or four) in softcover format; at the end of the year research
libraries send out those softcover issues to a bookbinder to
have them bound into a hard cover book that will last. A documentation entry therefore must include both volume and
issue number. As well, journals can have their pages numbered
in two ways: each issue can begin with page 1, or journals can
be continuously paginated throughout the year, with the first
page of each new issue following the last page of the previous
issue. There is a different APA entry for each type.

Here's an entry for an article in a journal with continuous
pagination throughout the year:

Last name, initial. (Year). Title of article. *Title of Journal,
Volume*, pages.

Leighton, B. (1991). Visions of community policing: Rhetoric and reality in Canada. *Canadian Journal of Criminology, 33*, 485–522.

And here's an entry for an article in a journal paginated by issue:

Last name, initial. (Year). Title of article. *Title of Journal, Volume*(issue), pages.

Leighton, B. (2006). Re-visions of community policing: Reality redefined for Canada. *Canadian Law Enforcement Quarterly, 27*(3), 12–23.

Internet sources are another category of documentation. The basic idea of supplying a URL is to allow the reader to get to the exact page on the Internet that you used. Because of the myriad of sources on the Internet, ranging from blogs to peer-reviewed online journals, selecting a style for an Internet entry is tricky. The information at www.apastyle.org/elecref.html contains a guide to APA for electronic sources.

Here is a basic format:

Last name, initial. (Year). *Title.* Date retrieved from website address

Valentino, L. (2007). APA *documentation.* Retrieved May 8, 2007, from www.humber.ca/valentin/apadoc.html

A Few Final Things to Consider

- Be sure to give an in-text citation within your essay (Ashworth, 2005).
- Ensure the reader can make the connection between the in-text citation and the full entry on the References page.
- Alphabetize your References page by author's last name.
- Don't forget to indent second and subsequent lines of entries.

EXPLORATIONS

10.1 Create an APA in-text reference for this text.

10.2 Create an APA bibliography entry for this text.

10.3 Create a reference page that includes each of the following types of entries:
- A book with one author
- A book with two or more authors
- An article in a collection
- An article in a journal paginated by issue
- An article in a journal paginated throughout the year

Appendix A

Writing for the Job Search: Résumés and Cover Letters

Throughout this text we have been looking at the types of writing done on the job by police officers. Let us now take a brief look at the writing involved in getting hired as an officer in the first place, specifically writing a résumé and cover letter.

A résumé is a summary of your education, experience, and skills that would be of interest to an employer. The following sample résumé modifies a résumé template available from Microsoft Office.

A résumé is reinforced by a cover letter that highlights your ability to contribute to an organization. The example following this résumé utilizes the matching letter template from Microsoft Office for a sample cover letter.

Rehnquist Résumé

```
                    CAROL REHNQUIST
                   432 South Millway
                  Mississauga, Ontario
                        L4S 2M5
                  Phone: 905-255-6653
             E-mail: carol.rehnquist@gmail.com
```

Objective

To join a progressive, world-class policing service

Education

Ontario College Diploma in Police Foundations

Humber College Institute of Technology and Advanced Learning

Toronto, Ontario

June 2008

- President's Award for highest academic average in program

- Board of Governors Award for community service

Experience

Security Guard (January 2006–present)
Thorncrest Security Services
422 Hawthorn Blvd.
Mississauga, Ontario

Lacrosse Referee (2002–present)
Mississauga Lacrosse Association

Volunteer Experience

Toronto Victims Services (May 2003–present)
Habitat for Humanity (October 2005–present
Toronto Police Rovers (September 2006–June 2008)

Skills

- Strong communication and interpersonal skills

- Excellent teamwork skills

- Proven ability to work independently

Rehnquist Cover Letter

Carol Rehnquist
432 South Millway
Mississauga, Ontario
L4S 2M5

June 27, 2008

Sergeant Paul Armstrong
Peel Regional Police Service
Human Resources Department
4292 Credit Valley Blvd.
Mississauga Ontario
L4F 4D3

Dear Sergeant Armstrong:

As a recent graduate of Humber College's Police Foundations Program, I am submitting my résumé for consideration as a constable in the Peel Regional Police Service. Peel Regional Police Service has a well-deserved reputation as a progressive, innovative law enforcement organization, and I would be proud to become a member.

When I entered Humber College in fall 2005, I had determined to make a contribution to society through a community services career. During my first year in the Social Services Worker program, I realized that my years as a volunteer in Victims Services had created a special interest in criminal justice issues. I transferred the following year to the Police Foundations Program, where I achieved the highest academic average in my class.

While in the Police Foundations Program, I had the opportunity to take part in the Police Rovers program, a joint venture of Toronto Police Service and Humber College. Under the mentorship of Constable Paul Friedel, I assisted in community policing initiatives, and got an inside look at policing realities by participating in many ride-alongs. At the same time, I experienced the world of private policing through my employment with Thorncrest Security Services.

As you can see from the attached Fitness Adequacy Certificate, I have met the fitness standards of the Service. I am an avid runner and have completed two marathons. During my time at Humber I was exposed to weightlifting, which I continue to pursue as a hobby. I played lacrosse as a goalie from ages six through eighteen, and still referee on a regular basis.

Those who have worked with me, either at school, on the job, or in a volunteer setting, will attest to my interpersonal skills and ability to work as part of a team. I have strong communication skills; my written communication skills are demonstrated by my strong results in Humber's required writing courses.

I can be contacted by phone at 905-255-6653 or by email at carol.rehnquist@gmail.com. I look forward to discussing the possibility of my putting my interest and enthusiasm to work for the benefit of the citizens of Peel region.

Sincerely,

Carol Rehnquist

Carol Rehnquist

Appendix B

Grammar, Spelling, and Mechanics

The following is a brief review of a few points of grammar and punctuation. If you are weak in grammar, punctuation, or spelling, your teacher might suggest a suitable text to help you improve your skills.

The Basics

Let's start with the building blocks of sentences: parts of speech. There are eight parts of speech:

1. nouns
2. verbs
3. adjectives
4. adverbs
5. prepositions
6. conjunctions
7. articles
8. interjections

Here is a brief description of each of these.

1. *Nouns* can be classified in several ways:

   - proper (the proper names of things, e.g., Saskatchewan, Lucy, Ottawa Renegades) and common (the class of objects, e.g., province, person, team)

   - concrete (objects, e.g., table, clock, house) and abstract (concepts, e.g., love, justice, peace)

   - count (things that can be counted, e.g., knife, finger, tree) and non-count (things that can't be counted, e.g., sugar, air, music)

2. *Verbs* can also be thought of in different ways:

- verbs are either transitive (taking an object, e.g., hit the ball), intransitive (not taking an object, e.g., sneeze), or copulative (sometimes called linking, e.g., is, seems)
- verbs have four principal parts (*base form* or *infinitive*, e.g., to sing, to play; *past*, e.g., sang, played; *past participle*, e.g., have sung, have played; *present participle*, e.g., am singing, am playing)
- verbs have different forms depending on:

a. tense
   - present (talk)
   - past (talked)
   - future (will talk)
   - present perfect (have talked)
   - past perfect (had talked)
   - future perfect (will have talked)
   - present progressive (am talking)
   - past progressive (was talking)
   - future progressive (will be talking)
   - present perfect progressive (have been talking)
   - past perfect progressive (had been talking)
   - future perfect progressive (will have been talking)

b. person (first: I, we; second: you; third: he, she, it, they)

c. number (singular, plural)

d. mood (indicative: making a statement; imperative: giving a command; subjunctive: hypothetical situations, situations contrary to fact, and so on)

e. voice (active: the subject of the sentence performs the action; passive: the subject of the sentence is acted upon)

3. *Adjectives* modify nouns or pronouns
4. *Adverbs* modify verbs, adjectives, and adverbs

---

5. *Prepositions* are used in prepositional phrases to signal time (after the game), space (under the car), or exclusion (everyone but Anne)
6. *Conjunctions* are used to join words, phrases, or clauses; they are either coordinating or subordinating (see pages 204 and 205)
7. *Articles* come before nouns; there are two types:

   • definite (the): points to specific object (the table, the house, the old woman)

   • indefinite (a, an): points to generic object (a table, a house, an old woman)

8. *Interjections* are words or phrases interjected (tossed) into a sentence to express emotion (e.g., Yikes! Ouch! Oh dear!)

Why Are Parts of Speech Important?

Parts of speech are the building blocks of sentences. While one can certainly compose a sentence without knowing the names of parts of speech, it is difficult to eliminate errors if you lack a vocabulary that your teacher and other educated persons take for granted. It's hard to stop writing fragments, for instance, if you don't understand when your teacher tells you your sentence is missing a verb. While it doesn't often come up in day-to-day conversation, the ability to identify and understand parts of speech is a useful skill, and critical to error-free writing.

Basics of Sentence Structure

The base structure of all sentences is quite simple: noun or pronoun plus verb. This basic structure is referred to as subject plus predicate.

N + V
or
P + V

In some cases, the subject does not even need to be stated, but instead is understood.

> Listen!
> (You) Listen!

This base structure is an independent clause (IC). An independent clause can stand alone. It might be dull, it might be boring, but it is grammatically correct. A dependent clause (DC), on the other hand, cannot stand alone. It needs to be joined somehow to an independent clause if the sentence is to be grammatically correct.

Let's look at the following sentence:

> I went to the store.

"I" is the subject, "went" is the verb (or predicate), and "to the store" is a prepositional phrase modifying the verb (telling where I went).

Suppose I want to give more information. Why did I go to the store?

> I went to the store. I was out of milk.

This is correct, but it sounds childish. These two sentences can be combined with a conjunction.

> I went to the store because I was out of milk.

"Because" is a *subordinating conjunction*, making the part of the sentence it introduces dependent on the rest of the sentence for its meaning. Look what happens if that part of the sentence is left to stand alone:

> Because I was out of milk.

Well? What happened because I was out of milk? What did I do because I was out of milk? The dependent clause makes little sense by itself; it requires the rest of the sentence for its meaning to be clear. (This type of error is called a *fragment*, since it is an incomplete sentence.)

Another type of conjunction is a *coordinating conjunction*. "Co" means equal; the two parts of a sentence joined by a coordinating conjunction could exist by themselves and still make sense.

> I was out of milk and I went to the store.

"And" is a coordinating conjunction (the others are *but*, *for*, *so*, and *yet*).

How about this sentence?

> I was out of milk; therefore, I went to the store.

"Therefore" is not a conjunction, but something called a *conjunctive adverb*. It does show the logical connection between two parts of a sentence, but it does not have the grammatical power to join them by itself; it requires a semicolon to finish the job.

If I were to write

> I was out of milk, therefore, I went to the store.

I would have written a *comma splice*: two sentences masquerading as one.

Sentence Types

There are four sentences types:

1. A *simple* sentence consists of one independent clause; that is, a subject and a verb, along with any associated modifiers or prepositional phrases.

IC

> I spoke to Juerg's sister yesterday.

2. A *compound* sentence consists of two or more independent clauses joined by a coordinating conjunction.

IC coordinating conjunction IC

> I spoke to Juerg's sister yesterday, but I haven't seen her today.

3. A *complex* sentence consists of a dependent clause plus an independent clause. The dependent clause may include a subordinating conjunction.

DC, IC

> Although I haven't seen Juerg in weeks, I spoke to his sister yesterday.

or
IC, DC

> I spoke to Juerg's sister yesterday, although I haven't seen him in weeks.

4. A *compound-complex* sentence is a combination of the two types, consisting of one or more dependent clauses and one or more independent clauses.

DC, IC coordinating conjunction IC

> Although I haven't seen Juerg in weeks, I spoke to his sister yesterday, and she said he was fine.

or
IC coordinating conjunction IC, DC

> I spoke to Juerg's sister yesterday, but I haven't seen her today because she went out of town.

Subject–Verb Agreement

A singular subject takes a singular verb; a plural subject takes a plural verb.

> The *boy rides* his bike.
>
> The *boys ride* their bikes.

Notice that a verb in third-person singular ends in *s*. (I ride, you ride, he rides, we ride, you ride, they ride).

Pronouns such as everyone, everybody, anyone, someone, and somebody are considered singular.

Pronoun Agreement

A pronoun stands for a noun (its antecedent). A singular antecedent takes a singular pronoun; a plural antecedent takes a plural pronoun. (Boy—his; boys—their.)

The tricky part here is dealing with the indefinite pronouns that are considered singular, mentioned under subject–verb agreement. Technically speaking, the following sentence is correct:

> Everyone should bring his own paper to the test.

In speaking, however, we commonly use a plural possessive pronoun for these indefinite pronouns. In writing, a singular pronoun is still correct, but for how long is anyone's guess.

Punctuation

Apostrophe

Another common source of errors is apostrophes. Some people sprinkle apostrophes liberally in their writing, letting them fall where they may, whereas others leave them out altogether. Neither practice is correct.

The apostrophe has two uses: to form *contractions* and to show *possession*.

> **Contractions:**
> would not—wouldn't
> do not—don't
> cannot—can't
> you are—you're
> it is—it's

Notice that the apostrophe in a contraction is placed wherever letters have been dropped. It is not placed haphazardly but, instead, stands for the missing letters.

> **Possession:**
> the coat belonging to the boy—the boy's coat
> the coats belonging to the boys—the boys' coats
> the coats belonging to them—their coats
> the fur belonging to the cat—the cat's fur
> the fur belonging to it (the cat)—its fur

Notice that possessive pronouns do not take an apostrophe (*their, its, your*). If you add an apostrophe to *its*, as in *it's*, the meaning of the word changes to "it is."

Comma

The comma has five main uses (other than in dates, addresses, and so on):

1. between items in a series

> For the party I bought red, green, yellow, blue, and purple balloons.

2. between independent clauses joined by a coordinating conjunction

> I tried to get pink balloons, but they were sold out.

3. after an introductory clause

> Since the pink balloons were sold out, I decided to return the pink streamers.

4. around anything that gets between the subject and verb

> The salesperson, however, told me the pink balloons would be in on Tuesday.

5. after a conjunctive adverb

> The party isn't until Friday; therefore, I'll go back Wednesday for pink balloons.

Proofreading

Proofreading sounds easy. Simply read over what you've written, and fix the mistakes, right? Unfortunately, it's not that simple, and the reason lies in our brain's ability to overlook what it does not expect. Find the mistake in this sentence:

> I called up Phil and we made plans to meet at the Tim Hortons at the the corner of Adelaide and Main.

Did you find it? Chances are good that your brain simply ignored the second "the" in that sentence. And that's what makes proofreading difficult. Our brains are really good at compensating for minor errors. In order to proofread effectively, we need to outsmart the brain. Here are two tips:

1. *Try proofreading backwards*. I start with the last sentence of my writing, and proofread backward, one sentence at a time, moving upward through the page. This seems to circumvent the brain's tendency to blind me to errors. Because I'm doing something out of the ordinary, starting at the end and moving to the beginning, rather than starting at the top and cruising down, I am able to see what is actually on the page.

2. *Keep an error log*. Out of the multitude of errors a person could make, each of us seems to have our personal tendencies. While it is important to do a global proofread, looking for all errors, it is helpful to follow that with a proofread that focuses on your most common mistakes. In order to do that personal proofread, we first need to analyze the patterns of our errors. Go back to pieces of writing you have done throughout your academic career. What types of errors do you seem to have a fondness for? Which types of things have you had to look out for in your rough drafts? What types of corrections have your teachers made?

Get a small notebook, and log the errors. Step back and look at the patterns. Do you usually spell *receive* as *recieve*? Do you tend to put apostrophes in verbs, or overuse commas? Do you confuse *their* and *there*? What are your recurring errors?

Once you've done the analysis, the rest is simple. Each time you write something, do a global proofread, and then check for your personal errors. And each time you get marked writing back, go back to your error log and update it if necessary.

By paying attention to your personal errors, you may be able to eliminate them for good. If you can't, though—because bad habits are incredibly hard to break—you'll at least be able to ensure that those errors aren't there by the time someone else reads your work.

A Note on Grammar and Spell Checkers

Word processing software now includes grammar- and spell-check functions. If you write with a computer, be sure to use them, but use them with caution. Both grammar checkers and spell checkers offer useful suggestions, but they are not fool-proof, and they are no substitute for your own judgment. Always, ALWAYS, proofread!

Appendix C

Spelling: Sound-Alikes and Look-Alikes

The following are some of the most commonly confused words in the English language. Review them and always try to avoid making these mistakes in your writing.

accept   *Accept* means "take." It is always a verb.

except   *Except* means "excluding."

Everyone *except* Mia *accepted* my explanation.

---

advice   *Advice* (rhymes with *nice*) is a noun.

advise   *Advise* (rhymes with *wise*) is a verb.

The difference in pronunciation makes the difference in meaning clear.

I *advise* you not to listen to free *advice*.

---

affect   *Affect* as a verb means "influence." As a noun, it means "a strong feeling" (as also seen in a related word, *affection*).

effect   *Effect* is a noun meaning "result." If you can substitute *result*, then *effect* is the word you need. Occasionally, effect is used as a verb meaning "to bring about."

Learning about the *effects* of caffeine *affected* my coffee-drinking habits.

Depressed people often display inappropriate *affect*.

Antidepressant medications can *effect* profound changes in mood.

allusion   An *allusion* is an implied or indirect reference.

illusion   An *illusion* is something that appears to be real or true but it is not what it seems. It can be a false impression, idea, or belief.

Many literary *allusions* can be traced to the Bible or to Shakespeare.

A good movie creates an *illusion* of reality.

are   *Are* is a verb.

our   *Our* shows ownership.

Confusion of these two words often results from careless pronunciation.

Where *are our* leaders?

choose   Pronunciation gives the clue here. *Choose* rhymes with *booze* and means "select."

chose   *Chose* rhymes with *rose* and means "selected."

Please *choose* a topic.

I *chose* filmmaking.

cite   To *cite* means "to quote from" or "to refer to."

sight	*Sight* is the ability to see, or something that is visible or worth seeing.
site	A *site* is the location of something: a building, a town, or an historic event.

> A lawyer *cites* precedents; writers *cite* their sources in articles or research papers; and my friends *cite* my essays as examples of brilliant writing.
>
> She lost her *sight* as the result of an accident.
>
> With his tattoos and piercings, Izzy was a *sight* to behold.
>
> The *site* of the battle was the Plains of Abraham, which lies west of Quebec City.

coarse	*Coarse* means "rough, unrefined." (Remember: the slang word *arse* is co*arse*.)
course	For all other meanings, use *course*.

> That sandpaper is too *coarse* to use on the lacquer finish.
>
> *Coarse* language only weakens your argument.
>
> Of *course* you'll do well in a *course* on the history of pop music.

complement A *complement* completes something.

compliment A *compliment* is a gift of praise.

> A glass of wine would be the perfect *complement* to the meal.
>
> Some people are embarrassed by *compliments*.

conscience   Your *conscience* is your sense of right and wrong.

conscious   *Conscious* means "aware" or "awake" (able to feel and think).

After Ann cheated on the test, her *conscience* bothered her.

Ann was *conscious* of having done wrong.

The injured man was *unconscious*.

---

consul   A *consul* is a government official stationed in another country.

council   A *council* is an assembly or official group.

counsel   Members of a *council* are *councillors*. *Counsel* can be used to mean both "advice" and "to advise."

The Canadian *consul* in Venice was very helpful.

The Women's Advisory *Council* meets next month.

Maria gave me good *counsel*.

She *counselled* me to hire a lawyer.

---

desert   A *desert* (with the emphasis on the first *e*) is a dry, barren place.

dessert   As a verb, *desert* means "leave behind." *Dessert* is the part of a meal that you'd probably like a second helping of, so give it a double *s*.

> The tundra is Canada's only *desert* region.
>
> As soon as our backs were turned, our guard *deserted* his post.
>
> Ice cream is my children's favourite *dessert*.

forth   *Forth* means "forward."

fourth   *Fourth* contains the number *four*, which gives it its meaning.

> Please stop pacing back and *forth*.
>
> The Raptors lost their *fourth* game in a row.

hear   *Hear* is what you do with your ears.

here   *Here* is used for all other meanings.

> Now *hear* this!
>
> Ranjan isn't *here*.
>
> *Here* is your assignment.

it's   *It's* is a shortened form of *it is*. The apostrophe takes the place of the *i* in *is*. If you can substitute *it is*, then *it's* is the form you need. *It's* is also commonly used as the shortened form of *it has*. In this case, the apostrophe takes the place of the *h* and the *a*.

its   If you can't substitute *it is*, then *its* is the correct word.

> *It's* not really difficult. (*It is* not really difficult.)
>
> The book has lost *its* cover. ("The book has lost it is cover" makes no sense, so you need *its*.)
>
> *It's* been a bad month for software sales.

later   Later refers to time and has the word *late* in it.

latter   Latter means "the second of two" and has two t's. It is the opposite of *former*.

It is *later* than you think.

You take the former, and I'll take the *latter*.

---

lead   Lead is pronounced to rhyme with *speed* and is the present tense of the verb *to lead*.

led   Led is the past tense of the same verb. The only time you pronounce *lead* as "led" is when you are referring to the soft, heavy, grey metal used to make bullets or leaded windows.

You *lead*, and I'll decide whether to follow.

Your suitcase is so heavy it must be filled with either gold or *lead*.

---

loose   Pronunciation is the key to these works. Loose rhymes with *goose* and means "not tight."

lose   Lose rhymes with *ooze* and means "misplace" or "be defeated."

A *loose* electrical connection is dangerous.

Some are born to win, some to *lose*.

---

moral   Again, pronunciation provides the clue you need. Moral refers to the understanding of what is right and wrong.

morale   Morale refers to the spirit or mental condition of a person or group.

Most religions are based on a *moral* code of behaviour.

Despite his shortcomings, he is basically a *moral* man.

Low *morale* is the reason for our employee's absenteeism.

personal	*Personal* means "private."
personnel	*Personnel* refers to the group of people working for a particular employer or to the office responsible for maintaining employees' records.

The letter was marked "*Personal* and Confidential."

We are fortunate to have highly qualified *personnel*.

Yasmin works in the *Personnel* Office.

principal	*Principal* means "main."
principle	A *principle* is a rule.

A *principal* is the main administrator of a school.

The federal government is Summerside's *principal* employer.

The *principal* and the interest totalled more than I could pay. (In this case, "the principal" is the main amount of money.)

One of the instructor's *principles* is to refuse to accept late assignments.

quiet	If you pronounce these words carefully, you won't confuse them. *Quiet* has two syllables.
quite	*Quite* has only one.

> The chairperson asked us to be *quiet*.
>
> We had not *quite* finished our assignment.

than   *Than* is used in comparisons. Pronounce it to rhyme with *can*.

then   *Then* refers to time and rhymes with *when*.

> Karim is a better speller *than* I am.
>
> He made his decision *then*.
>
> Tanya withdrew from the competition; *then* she realized the consequences.

their   *Their* indicates ownership.

there   *There* points out something or indicates place. It includes the word *here*, which also indicates place.

they're   *They're* is a shortened form of *they are*. (The apostrophe replaces the *a* in *are*.)

> It was *their* fault.
>
> *There* are two weeks left in the term.
>
> Let's walk over *there*.
>
> *They're* late, as usual.

too   The *too* with an extra *o* means "more than enough" or "also."

two   *Two* is the number after one.

to   For all other meanings, use *to*.

She thinks she's been working *too* hard. He thinks so *too*.

There are *two* sides *to* every argument.

The *two* women knew *too* much about each other *to* be friends.

---

were   If you pronounce these three carefully, you won't confuse them. *Were* rhymes with *fur* and is a verb.

where   *Where* is pronounced "hwear," includes the word *here*, and indicates place.

we're   *We're* is a shortened form of *we are* and is pronounced "weer."

You *were* joking, *weren't* you?

Where did you want to meet?

We're on our way.

---

who's   *Who's* is a shortened form of *who is* or *who has*. If you can substitute *who is* or *who has* for the *who's* in your sentence, then you have the right spelling.

whose   Otherwise, use *whose*.

Who's coming to dinner? (*Who is* coming to dinner?)

Who's been sleeping in my bed? (*Who has* been sleeping in my bed?)

Whose paper is this? ("*Who is* paper" makes no sense, so you need *whose*.)

you're *You're* is a shortened form of *you are*. If you can substitute *you are* for *you're* in your sentence, then *you're* using the correct form.

your If you can't substitute *you are*, use *your*.

You're welcome. (*You are* welcome.)

Unfortunately, *your* hamburger got burned. ("*You are* hamburger" makes no sense, so *your* is the word you want.)

Index